Russell Gr

Teaching on a
Shoestring

An A–Z of everyday objects to enthuse and engage
children and extend learning in the early years

Crown House Publishing Limited
www.crownhouse.co.uk

First published by
Crown House Publishing Ltd
Crown Buildings, Bancyfelin, Carmarthen, Wales, SA33 5ND, UK
www.crownhouse.co.uk

and

Crown House Publishing Company LLC
PO Box 2223, Williston, VT 05495, USA
www.crownhousepublishing.com

British Library of Cataloguing-in-Publication Data

A catalogue entry for this book is available from the British Library.

Print ISBN: 978-178583307-6
Mobi ISBN: 978-178583359-5
ePub ISBN: 978-178583360-1
ePDF ISBN: 978-178583361-8

LCCN 2018946209

Printed and bound in the UK by
Gomer Press, Llandysul, Ceredigion

Contents

Introduction

All things bright and beautiful

Margaret Woodbury Strong (1897–1969) was a rather eccentric American who once lined her garden boundary with forty bathtubs filled with flowers. Her wealthy father was an avid collector and on family holidays all over the world she was given a small bag to collect toys, dolls and other small objects. By the time she was an old lady, Margaret had acquired 22,000 dolls among more than 3,000,000 household objects, spread over fifty categories such as sport, holidays and music. The objects included buttons, shells, paperweights, glassware and kitchen appliances, although most of her collections related in some way to children's play. When Margaret died, she left enough funds to open a 'Museum of Fascination' (now called 'The Strong') which includes the National Toy Hall of Fame. Visiting the museum has been likened to being let loose in Santa's workshop on a day in December before the sleigh departs. The Strong is packed full of toys and games that have sustained their popularity over the years, such as yo-yos, puzzles and action figures.

In 2005, however, a rather mundane object was added to the National Toy Hall of Fame – the cardboard box. Undoubtedly one of the most versatile of objects, the cardboard box captures children's imaginations across the world – within a few minutes, boxes are transformed into forts, houses, submarines, castles, caves and spaceships. Smaller boxes become doll's house furniture, while larger boxes are turned into television screens or refrigerators. The cardboard box represents a refreshing change from conspicuous spending, as anxious parents seek to acquire 'the latest thing' for their children. A recent survey of

Figure 1. The humble cardboard box

2,000 parents of children aged three and above found that at Christmas time 46% of children prefer playing with boxes instead of actual toys and games, although parents feel pressurised to spend more than £200 on 'must have' items (Davis, 2012; Trajectory, 2012). The reality is that children can derive considerable pleasure and intellectual stimulation without expensive things. Observe any child playing on the beach, in the garden, at home or in the classroom, and you will soon see examples of how their creativity, enthusiasm and communication flourishes by engaging with the very simple objects at hand – pebbles, leaves, tubes, old clothes, pipes, hats, pallets, cloths, hand-bags, steering wheels, egg boxes and suitcases.

This is a book about the educational potential of everyday objects. It is aimed at early years practitioners, students on education courses, parents and those who work in museums and galleries. In the introduction, we provide an overview of objects in society so that readers are well informed when they hold discussions with children linked to the practical activities in Part 2. We believe passionately that the educational potential of objects increases when they are related to people – those individuals that made and used the objects.

Think about the popular television programme, *Antiques Roadshow*. Once the owner and presenter begin to discuss the stories behind the objects, we are drawn into their worlds and the emotions this brings – whether sadness, surprise, laughter or anger. To mark the 100th anniversary of the First World War, the show's producers launched an appeal for people to tell their stories of wartime objects. This resulted in an astonishing response from viewers. Among the poignant objects was a 1914 Christmas dinner menu for soldiers in the trenches signed by all those who were present and William Bell's erroneous death certificate. Bell, a sergeant from Liverpool, was reported to have been killed in action in 1918 and his wife received the dreaded telegram to that effect. Imagine how she must have felt on reading the telegram. Then imagine her reaction when he returned home in 1919. He kept the certificate, despite pressure from the army authorities to return it, saying he would dine out on the story for the rest of his life. Billy lived on until 1975. Many of the objects featured on the programme are now unusual or rare but they were once commonplace.

When discussing mundane, familiar objects with children, it is worth bearing in mind that one day in the future these may become antiques. Michael Hogben (2007), a leading antiques trader, has identified 101 everyday objects which he considers will be highly collectable in the future. These include chunky digital wristwatches from the 1970s, McDonald's toys from the 1990s and the earliest mobile phones, first used by the general public in 1982.

The meaning and significance of objects

A simple definition of an object is a natural or artificial item that can be seen and touched. Many everyday objects define who we are. Some sociologists argue that it is possible to determine your social class from the household objects you own.[1] Etiquette expert William Hanson (2015) has identified the kind of objects that would typically feature in an upper middle class home. The kitchen would include an Aga cooker, a cling film dispenser, cups and saucers (rather than mugs and a mug tree) and no coasters. Ask a group of children to match objects to occupations and most can do this without much difficulty.[2] Everyday objects have meaning when we use them – we sleep in beds, we use knives and forks to eat, and pens or computers to write.

Objects are produced and used by people at a given time in society and so have social meaning. They reflect our ideas and ideals. Think about the objects in your own home and what they say about your interests, values and relationships. The long running television programme *Through the Keyhole* invites a panel of celebrities to guess the identities of reasonably famous people after a virtual tour of their homes and what clues the household items reveal. The programme's appeal lies in our curiosity and desire to find out about the lives of other people. The objects are a means to this end. When objects are shared they take on a social purpose – they govern or inform interactions. As gifts, objects often strengthen bonds with family and friends.

---

1   There are online quizzes to this effect, e.g. http://www.thepoke.co.uk/2016/09/26/how-middle-class-are-you/.
2   You can find worksheets on this at: https://www.turtlediary.com/worksheet/match-objects-with-occupation.html.

Psychologists say that it is usually the giver, rather than the recipient, who gains the most socially and emotionally from a gift.

In *Snoop: What Your Stuff Says About You* (2009), the psychologist Sam Gosling argues that our household goods reveal our true personality more so than face-to-face discussions. Based on extensive research, Gosling concludes that the objects we collect and the environments we create are not simply about sending messages to others but are there to help us manage our thoughts and emotions. He refers to family photos, CDs and even the colour of the walls as 'feeling regulators', helping us to focus on what is important or to reminisce about former times.

It is increasingly recognised that objects have an important role to play in helping isolated elderly people to communicate and make sense of their lives. Research shows that many old people in sheltered accommodation come to terms with their surroundings through caring for objects and images linked to their memories (Rowlands, 2008). In their experiments across Europe and the United States, British psychologists Gregory Jones and Maryanne Martin (2006) asked participants, 'If you could save one object from a fire, what would you save?' The responses showed that the objects people would save were those which evoked strong memories like photographs, jewellery, ornaments and childhood toys rather than laptops and other expensive items. Objects have been used successfully to care for and spark the memories of those who suffer from dementia. For example, the experience of looking through photographs and handling artefacts has helped people to remember things, become less frustrated and to eat more. In short, possessing objects can contribute to people's well-being. And, of course, objects support intergenerational learning. They can become a focal point for building conversations and relationships between the young and the old (Thomas, 2009).

Children have always had an interest in objects, particularly toys. Beginning in 1918, Charles Quennell and his wife, Marjorie, wrote a landmark series called A History of Everyday Things in England. In the introduction to their first book, the Quennells apologised for providing only a sketch history due to 'a shortage of paper' (paper, which we take for granted, was rationed during the First World War) but called on schoolchildren to explore everyday things around them (Quennell and Quennell, 1918: x). Their illustrated series brought joy to many young and old readers alike who learned how things worked, from hair-cutting in the twelfth century to the new 20-inch televisions of the late 1950s – interference was a major hazard when a passing car produced electrical disturbances that made the screen 'look like a firework display' (Ellacott, 1968: 166). The significance of objects is summed up by the fact that they define historical ages; we refer to prehistoric people as living in the Stone Age while we think of ourselves as living in the Computer Age.

Age of abundance

We are living in what some historians and social commentators call an 'Age of Abundance' (Lindsey, 2008; see also Diamandis and Kotler, 2012). Before the Industrial Revolution and the mass production of goods, even a quite prosperous family house would have had few possessions – the main room typically containing only a table, benches, a chair and a cupboard (Flanders, 2014). Certainly, things we take for granted today were once viewed very differently. Take the example of a shirt or coat. In his breathtaking book, *The Empire of Things*, the historian Frank Trentmann (2016) explains how in the past a coat was not discarded until its fibres were literally coming apart. Another historian has suggested that a medieval shirt would have cost US$3,500 (around £2,600) to produce, based on a staggering 579 hours of labour – sewing, weaving and spinning.[3] Today, one storage company found that the average Brit has fifty-eight items of clothing but only wears a third of them, and the average woman has seventeen pairs of shoes (men have eight) but regularly wear only six.[4]

Academics describe how we have lost the 'stewardship of objects' (Strasser, 2000) once held by our ancestors who valued the time and effort it took to make things. A culture of make do and mend has been replaced by a culture of disposal. The trend over recent decades has been to use more and more

---

3   The calculations have been challenged but the main point – that items were a lot more expensive – remains valid. See http://www.bradford-delong.com/2016/08/weekend-reading-eve-fisher-the-3500-shirt-a-history-lesson-in-economics.html.

4   See https://www.storefirst.com/storage-news/a-nation-of-hoarders-figures-reveal-brits-are-wasting-two-thirds-of-their-wardrobes-on-rarely-worn-clothes/.

disposable items – cups, cameras, razors and so on. Unfortunately, this has serious environmental implications. To illustrate, it is estimated that if all our useless and discarded Christmas presents were combined they would cover 48.7 square miles – an area greater than the size of Edinburgh (Clearabee, 2015)! The typical home contains £1,000 worth of unused clutter (*Daily Mail*, 2013a). In short, most of us have too much stuff. The move from the age of scarcity to the age of abundance has meant that we are surrounded by millions of things. At a click of a button, it's possible to access goods from all over the world.

But does the possession of lots of objects make us more contented? A recent US study (Weidman and Dunn, 2016) compared how people reacted to material and experiential purchases for two weeks, up to five times in a day. The material purchases included items such as a tablet computer, while examples of experiential purchases included weekend trips or tickets to a basketball game. Results suggest that material and experiential purchases both deliver happiness but in different ways. Material purchases provide more *frequent* momentary happiness over time, whereas experiential purchases provide more *intense* momentary happiness on individual occasions.

But there is no doubt that young children are exposed to messages which equate happiness with material possessions. One US researcher examined thirty picture books for young children and found that they featured 'excessive amounts of toys, sending pro-consumer messages to children aged zero to six' (Flood, 2013). In one wordless picture book, *A Ball for Daisy* (Raschka, 2015), the dog (Daisy) loves her ball, only to see it broken by another dog. Daisy plunges into sadness, but her happiness returns when she is given a new ball the next day. The researcher concludes that the unfortunate message for children in this and other stories is that happiness is dependent upon objects.

Companies target children with great success, so much so that by the age of three some children recognise McDonald's Golden Arches before they can say their own surname. We know that three- and four-year-olds are brand savvy (Watkins et al., 2016). By the age of ten, UK children know around 350 brands. Children from a very young age are subjected to and exert their own pressures to get more things. The marketing industry fully recognises this – targeting child consumers as 'preteens', 'tweenies' and 'tinies'. Given that barely fifty years ago there was no such thing as a teenage market, perhaps it is not stretching the imagination too far to envisage in a few years' time a marketplace of objects for the yet-to-be-born – 'foeties' or 'wombies'. The *Daily Mail* (2013b) cheerfully reports, 'Hello baby! Incredible 3D scans allow parents to see foetus SMILING' and 'Incredible 4D ultrasound scans show what foetuses REALLY get up to in the womb' (Blott, 2016). For the teaching profession and parents, what really matters is teaching young children moral values and critical thinking skills, so they see happiness as less contingent upon material things and more closely associated with cultivating relationships.

There is a danger of too readily reaching the gloomy conclusion that modern Britain has become a consumerist, materialistic society that only values what a person owns, and that success in life is seen to be about acquiring more and more of the latest things and showing them off to impress peers. Not everyone agrees with this analysis (e.g. Ormerod, 2016). An increasing number of everyday items – newspapers, music, books, films – are not being bought for *ownership*; rather, more and more people are accessing the media online instead of in tangible forms. Moreover, although consumer spending is increasing, economists point out that the market strengths lie in entertainment and travel (despite the global threat of terrorism). In short, it is argued that *experiences* are becoming more important than things. However, the argument becomes less convincing when you consider hard facts and figures – for example, the typical US household has 300,000 things (MacVean, 2014) and is consuming twice as much as they did fifty years ago (Taylor and Tilford, 2000), while the average ten-year-old in Britain owns 238 toys but plays regularly with only a handful (*The Telegraph*, 2010).

Objects and sustainability

In the modern world, advanced economies are characterised by the increasing production of short-term, disposable items, culminating in the notion of the 'throwaway society'. This term, first used in the 1950s, has become almost redundant given that few remember what it was like to live at a time when people routinely repaired things and products lasted a lifetime. As the journalist Jenny McCartney (2013) points out: 'Nothing in modern life lasts as long as it used to: relationships, news reports, hairstyles, attention spans, gadgetry, shoes or clothes.' One enterprising businesswoman has set up her own company (www.buymeonce.com) which offers products made to last a lifetime, like the Fisher space pen which claims to write for so long that the average user won't run out of ink during their entire life – a mere snip at £155. Most people will, of course, buy cheap biros – a box of fifty costs less than £4. Economists use the term 'planned obsolescence' to describe manufacturers' deliberate intention to limit the shelf life (e.g. functionality or appeal) of products so that people buy more. Moreover, many products are expensive to repair and it is almost cheaper to replace a broken toaster or kettle with a new one than it is to try to fix it. Families also spend less time cooking at home using fresh ingredients, instead relying more on packaged, processed meals.

A bottle of mineral water is a good example of an object which illustrates the change in how we live. Until the twentieth century, a constant supply of piped water was considered a domestic luxury. In previous centuries, most people bought water from the barrels of street water carriers or drew water from street fountains and pumps, or from rivers, wells and springs. Although water has been bottled since the sixteenth century, companies such as Schweppes had taken this to a commercial scale by the 1900s. Demand has increased significantly over recent decades – sales of bottled water have increased from 800 million litres in 1995 to 2.8 billion litres in 2015.[5]

Figure 2. Bottled water – a good thing?

5   See http://www.aqbottledwater.com/hotel-bottled-water/new-consumer-health-trends-lead-way-bottled-water-sales/.

The industry is worth more than £2 billion. Why do increasing numbers of people prefer bottled rather than tap water? In her book, *Bottlemania* (2008), Elizabeth Royte points out that 99% of UK tap water is of a high standard (by 2014 the figure had risen to 99.96%), and yet tap water costs 0.1 penny per litre compared to around 85 pence for a litre of bottled water. Moreover, studies tell us that most people can't tell the difference between tap and branded bottled water in blind tests – try such a test with children. It seems that people buy bottled water for reasons other than taste. Perhaps it is the misconception that bottled water is healthier than tap water.

Whatever the reason, the environmental impact of using bottled water is staggering. It is estimated that British households fail to recycle 16 million plastic bottles each day, out of the 35 million which are used and discarded daily. The annual beach clean-up undertaken by the Marine Conservation Society typically collects 8,000 plastic bottles. The campaign group Recycle Now estimates that it takes 500 years for a plastic bottle to break down once in the sea (see Smithers, 2016).

Fundamentally, what is needed is the political will and popular support to move from a linear (make–use–dispose) to a circular (make–keep–recover–regenerate) economy. Leading academics argue that such a transformation would represent an alternative to the throwaway society and bring social, economic and environmental gains. For instance, forecasts suggest better value for money, greater consumer satisfaction and more jobs in the repair and maintenance industry (Cooper, 2010). Put simply, if we created fewer but better quality products, looked after them carefully and invested more in repair, renovation and upgrading, then the environmental savings would be huge.

The good news is that over the past sixty or so years there have been concerted efforts to educate children and young people about living more sustainably. What is clear is that children need to engage directly with environmental issues rather than passively absorb information (Rickinson et al., 2004; RSPB, 2006). There is no doubt that campaigns such as 'reduce, reuse, recycle' have raised awareness among children and the general public about the importance of sustainability and a greener future. Around 34,000 schools in the UK take part in recycling schemes and there are many resources available to teachers to promote aspects of environmental education such as recycling.[6]

Interestingly, despite higher prices, more and more people are buying eco-friendly products. A major survey of 29,000 Internet respondents across fifty-eight countries shows that one in four UK consumers are choosing more environmentally friendly products (Retail Gazette, 2013). There are also positive community developments such as the Library of Things in Norwood, south-east London (www.libraryofthings.co.uk) and SHARE in Frome (https://sharefrome.org), where for a small fee people borrow things – from baking tins to carpet cleaners. Many of the objects featured in this book can be reused or recycled. Cardboard boxes, for example, can be reused for storage (especially if moving house) or as toy boxes. And, of course, generations of teachers have reused cardboard boxes in craft projects. Among the more creative ideas are desk organisers, paint palettes, cardboard photo frames, hats and weed barriers.

Although we live in a highly disposable age, it is also true that many of us enjoy collecting things – although this can be taken to extremes. According to the British Heart Foundation, which runs charity shops on the high street, eight out of ten Britons describe themselves as a hoarder. They admit to having junk at home which they have not touched for a decade (Kolirin, 2014). When asked why, the most popular response is, 'I hate throwing things away because you never know when you might need them again.' Kolirin listed the top ten most hoarded objects as follows:

1   Now CDs (30%)

2   Bread maker (25%)

3   Rubik's Cube (21%)

4   Lava lamp (19%)

5   Walkman (17%)

6   Gameboy (17%)

7   Beanie Babies (12%)

8   SodaStream (9%)

---

6   See e.g. http://www.recycling-guide.org.uk/schools.html.

9   Furby (8%)

10 Roller blades (8%)

Hoarding has its health risks. At an extreme it can lead to what psychologists call 'clutter disorder', which describes the mental and emotional anxiety people suffer when living with an overwhelming number of objects. In fact, the charity HoardingUK (https://hoardinguk.org) has worked with Oxford University to develop a Clutter Index Rating – a test can be completed online to assess your hoarding tendency. It seems that we all have an insatiable desire for more stuff. The US writer Barry Schwartz (2005) points out that as consumers we are faced with a paradox of choice. Manufacturers and retailers offer us so many different products that this creates 'choice overload', which can lead to dithering, anxiety and stress.

However, for most people collecting things represents an enjoyable pastime and many start at an early age. An online Mumsnet discussion on 'strange things kids collect' reveals collections of things such as pencil leads, bones, sticks, stones, elastic bands dropped by the postman, bottle tops and Horrible Science 'Slimy Aliens'.[7] Some things have stood the test of time, such as *Top Trumps*, first collected in the 1970s. One US academic paper found that children collect things because it satisfies their curiosity, relieves boredom and helps them to make friends (Baker and Gentry, 1996). Even the most mundane of everyday objects might one day become collectables. Most young children develop an attachment to a particular object, such as a teddy bear, toy or blanket. These hold positive memories for children, and so it is usual practice among nursery classes to encourage parents to bring these along to ease the transition from home to school.

---

7   https://www.netmums.com/coffeehouse/general-coffeehouse-chat-514/general-chat-18/468824-strange-things-kids-collect.html.

Adding value to objects

We take for granted many everyday objects. We owe a considerable debt to the likes of László Bíró, William Henry Hoover and Earl Silas Tupper, whose inventions – the commercial ballpoint pen, the vacuum cleaner and Tupperware – have become part of our daily lives. The stories behind such objects should be shared with young children because they often reveal qualities such as imagination, persistence and resourcefulness. Take the ubiquitous sticky note. What would life be like for teachers without it? In 1974, irritated by bookmarks that kept falling out of his hymn book, 3M researcher Arthur Fry played with the idea of using a sticky coating to retain his page marker. Within a few years, the Post-it note was developed and is now a global icon for quick and effective communication. Sticky notes have many uses in planning, creating and organising ideas. Figure 3 includes a few classroom examples.

Figure 3. Some classroom uses of sticky notes

It is possible to turn insignificant objects into significant ones without waiting for posterity. In 2009, a group of creative writers set up the Significant

Objects Project (www.significantobjects.com). They wanted to know whether they could make money by buying very cheap objects and telling a fictitious story around them in order to sell them on at a profit, so they decided to buy lots of things from bargain stores and eBay (Figure 4).

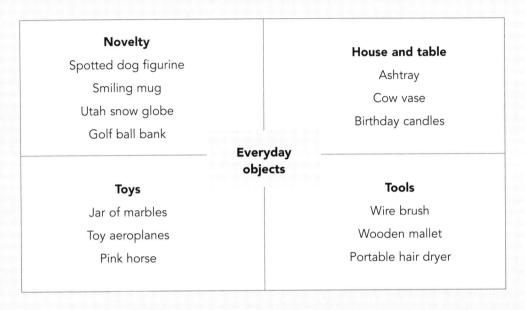

Novelty

Spotted dog figurine

Smiling mug

Utah snow globe

Golf ball bank

House and table

Ashtray

Cow vase

Birthday candles

Everyday objects

Toys

Jar of marbles

Toy aeroplanes

Pink horse

Tools

Wire brush

Wooden mallet

Portable hair dryer

Figure 4. Everyday items bought and then resold at major profit, as part of the Significant Objects Project

They wrote their stories and posted them alongside the objects for sale on eBay. In total, they sold US$128.74 worth of thrift-store junk for US$3,612.51. They subsequently repeated the experiment with even greater financial returns. The group then wrote a book on their project, *Significant Objects* (Walker and Glenn, 2012), which was named as one of the best design books of the year. This story illustrates that even the most mundane of objects can generate value and interest.

Summary

This preamble has tried to illustrate why everyday objects matter. They provoke sentiment, offer emotional security and define who we are as individuals and society at large. The meaning we attach to objects changes depending on the context. When we look at objects – rosary beads, a tennis ball, a screwdriver, the latest iPhone – we make assumptions about the owner's gender, age, interests, beliefs, dislikes and social and economic background. Objects raise big questions – for example, about prevailing political ideas and movements, social change and religious beliefs.

This is well illustrated by the work of a small team of curators at the Victoria and Albert Museum, who form what is called the Rapid Response team. Their job is to find contemporary objects for the museum which are of political, social and economic significance, and to display them to the public as quickly as possible. Among their recent findings have been an IKEA cuddly soft toy, a fake iPhone 5S and a 3D printed plastic gun (see Harrod, 2014). As one of the curators points out, each object has a story to tell about the world we live in today – whether this relates to working conditions in the Third World, political unrest in China or changing race relations. The IKEA toy, for example, symbolised dissatisfaction with the Chinese authorities when in December 2013 a citizen threw it at Leung Chun-Ying, the then chief executive of Hong Kong, during a town hall meeting. Leung was unpopular because of his association with the Chinese Communist Party. The choice of toy, a wolf called Lufsig, was significant. Leung's name in Chinese characters is like the character for 'wolf' and when transliterated into Chinese, Lufsig came out as an insult. The toy soon sold out in Hong Kong and it received more than 50,000 likes on one Facebook page.

This book focuses on the educational value of objects for young children. This has long been recognised. Susan Isaacs (1885–1948), a trained psychologist and former lecturer in infant school education at Darlington Training College, thought a great deal about the resources in her experimental nursery school in the 1920s. She equipped it with art and craft materials, beads, blocks, dressing-up clothes, a typewriter and outdoor resources for a playhouse, sandpit and tool shed. Settings founded on the work of Maria Montessori (1870–1952) use 'alphabet objects' to begin literacy work. The language starter set includes 100 miniatures such as animals and doll's house domestic objects like pots and pans.

We hope this book will inspire readers to think differently about everyday objects. In these tight economic times, practitioners, educational managers and leaders are ever mindful of 'value for money' principles when building up collections of resources. Put simply, this means spending less, spending well and spending wisely. Based on our travels around pre-school settings and primary schools, we have seen some exceptional practitioners teaching on a shoestring and trust that this book will help others to do so.

Organisation and use of this book

The book is organised into two parts. In Part 1, we consider the use of objects in the broader context of important questions about effective learning and teaching in the early years, which we apply to the under-sevens. It is widely acknowledged that the early years is a critical stage in children's development and predictive in terms of their future learning (Goodman et al., 2015). Many of the principles of object-based pedagogy we refer to can also be applied with older children. We consider how everyday objects can be used to develop four skills widely regarded as essential in the twenty-first century: communication, collaboration, critical thinking and creativity (the 4 C's; see also Appendix).

In Part 2, we select twenty-six everyday objects using an alphabetical format to illustrate how these skills can be taught. There is no special reason for choosing these particular objects – in fact, we hope that practitioners will choose objects from their own environment to suit their own needs. What matters is not so much the objects but the associated pedagogy – the quality of dialogue and other teaching skills, the relationships with the children and the learning climate that is created.

There is a common format for each object arranged into the following sections:

- **In a nutshell** – key background information about the object in its broader context.

- **Did you know?** – interesting facts about the object.

- **Ready** – resources, health and safety factors to consider and key vocabulary.

- **Steady** – learning goals and intentions to consider.

- **Go** – activities which show how teachers can develop the four skills of communication, collaboration, critical thinking and creativity around the object.

- **Other ideas** – follow-up cross-curricular ideas.

- **Find out more** – websites and other references for further information.

Part 1

Important questions

1. Why use objects when teaching in the early years?

One of the main reasons objects should be used in early years practice is that they have the potential to stimulate children's natural curiosity and creative thinking. Babies and toddlers use their senses to explore the physical, observable aspects of their immediate surroundings. The world is full of wonder and newness to investigate. This includes putting objects in their mouths, tapping and shaking things and responding to sounds – thereby gaining more experience and information. They reach out for objects such as mum's necklace, a bunch of keys or a pair of spectacles, which become absorbing play materials. As young children acquire language, they begin to ask questions about the many objects they see, hear, feel, taste and smell in their environments, both natural and built. This sense of wonder can be curtailed, however, through overly directive teaching, a prescribed assessment-led curriculum and an unstimulating learning environment. These factors can mitigate against children's creativity, with lessons reduced to a guessing game in which children try to figure out what answers the teacher wants.

Everyday objects should be used as teaching aids because they are excellent resources to support children's spiritual, moral, social and cultural development. Although physical by nature, objects can also have spiritual significance. Many individuals treasure objects from their childhood even though these may have been discarded by others long ago. Some objects, for whatever reason, become significant and personally valuable. They outlast individuals and are a means of bringing the past into the present, offering stability and continuity. Valerie Flournoy's classic story of *The Patchwork Quilt* (1985) gives young children a clear picture of how a simple quilt passed on from one generation to the next has meaning. Through stories, children can learn that objects are not only solid things (composed of physical matter) but also have symbolic value.

Skilled practitioners can bring a sense of awe into even the most familiar of objects. Take apples as an example (see 'A'). Some are the size of peas, others as large as small pumpkins; their colours range from yellow to lime green, chocolate brown and burgundy. Or what about that magical material that keeps birds warm and helps most of them fly? Feathers also have camouflage and display functions (see 'F'). One of the more unusual uses for feathers is to help birds grip as 'snow shoes' during winter months – feather-covered feet increase the size of the foot, which keeps the birds from sinking into snow. Woodpeckers use their feathers as supports while climbing trees, whereas Antarctic penguins cross the snow and ice using their smooth feathers in toboggan-style moves. Predators such as owls use their feathered ears as dishes to collect and channel sounds. These kinds of 'amazing facts' have always interested young children and older ones alike – consider the success of the Guinness World Records and Ripley's Believe It or Not!

There is also a moral dimension to the use of objects. Museum curators regularly face dilemmas over what objects to collect and exhibit. The most frequently asked question at the British Museum is 'Where are the mummies?' Is it morally justifiable to display human remains as objects of morbid curiosity? Does it promote voyeurism, or is it a commitment to share knowledge and generate interest in the past? The curators who lead on the Rapid Response team at the Victoria and Albert Museum are interested in collecting objects that reflect society 'warts and all' – and this includes products sold on the so-called 'dark web', the online market for illicit goods. This raises moral questions. Even a mundane object, such as a box of Katy Perry false eyelashes (£5.95 from Tesco), tells us something about a society in which Western teenage girls are encouraged to look like 'pop-cultural icons', while the product is 'knotted from human hair by women in a factory in Indonesia, paid as little as £50 per month'. The false lash industry has an estimated value of £110 million in Britain alone (Wainwright, 2014).

In Part 2, there are many opportunities to encourage young children to think about the moral dimension to the use of objects. For instance, is it right that some people take birds' eggs from the wild or pebbles from the beach (see 'E' and 'R')? There are also less clear-cut discussions to be held when considering the motives of characters in stories and the consequences of their actions – for example, is it ever right to take someone else's belongings? There are opportunities to explore the cultural significance of the objects discussed in Part 2. Feathers, for instance, can be used to create a First Nation American 'talking piece' for circle time.

Parents with links to countries around the world may be able to lend every-day objects and these can be grouped each week, so the class can explore similarities and differences. Even mundane holiday gifts such as fridge magnets can reveal information about national customs.

The cultural value of objects can also be seen in museum collections. Young children can learn much about the lives of people in the past by exploring objects. The Teaching History with 100 Objects project (www.teachinghistory100.org) is based on objects from museums in England, Northern Ireland, Scotland, Wales and the British Museum. For Key Stage 1, the objects include a bucket from the Great Fire of London and Florence Nightingale's writing case.

The skilful use of objects can help young children to acquire important skills in visual literacy – namely, interpretation and meaning making. Because children live in a media-rich age, the skill of being able to interpret images – photographs, webpages, films and objects – has taken on added significance. This is particularly so in a culturally diverse world where objects mean different things to different people across time and space. Gaynor Kavanagh (2000) illustrates this well through the story of four ordinary blankets from Wales, Glasgow, Lincolnshire and Belfast. While comparing the blankets can reveal similarities and differences in terms of colour, weave and signs of wear, it is only when the stories behind the blankets are told that we appreciate the human element.

The Welsh blanket was used by a woman to carry her baby and, as a hillside farmer, she needed her hands free to negotiate the difficult terrain. The Lincolnshire blanket was produced from a farm whose wool was sold to a wool merchant who, in turn, sold it to a Yorkshire mill. Eventually the blanket was returned to the Lincolnshire farm and kept as a tangible expression of its work. The story behind the Glasgow blanket is one of dire poverty during the nineteenth century. The owner pawned the blanket early in the morning and used the money to buy a basket of food. This was then sold during the day and some of the profit used to redeem the blanket from the pawnshop. Its purpose, then, was not so much to give warmth but to provide food. The Belfast blanket was used by Republican prisoners in the 1970s who refused to wear prison clothes but wrapped themselves in blankets instead.

Therefore, the same object can have very different meanings depending on the context.

2. How does the use of everyday objects fit with the requirements for the early years curriculum?

The use of objects aligns with the kind of practices that are officially endorsed in early years education. For instance, the government's Early Years Foundation Stage (EYFS) in England recognises that young children learn through playing and exploring, active learning, creating and thinking critically. Active learning is defined as 'learning in which the child, by acting on objects and interacting with people, ideas and events, constructs new understandings' (Hohmann and Weikart, 1995: 17). At other times, young children learn by being told how to do things and when adults use objects as visual aids. Think about children cooking where the adult models setting out the ingredients, the use of equipment or how to follow health and safety procedures. In their exploratory play, children might then make their own cakes out of play dough, using plastic cutters and decorating with glitter and small pieces of straw for 'candles'. Children also learn through trial and error, provided they are willing to have a go and try things out. They learn social skills by being with other people – their peers and adults.

While there are differences in the early years curricula throughout the United Kingdom (Table 1), notably in terms of age spans and the stand-alone nature of literacy in England, they share a commitment to providing young children with a broad range of stimulating learning experiences both indoors and outdoors. The emphasis is on making links between areas of learning.

Table 1. Areas of learning in the early years across the UK

Country	Area of learning
England: Early Years Foundation Stage (0–5)	Prime areas: ■ Communication and language ■ Physical development ■ Personal, social and emotional development Specific areas: ■ Literacy ■ Mathematics ■ Understanding the world ■ Expressive arts and design
Northern Ireland: Foundation Stage (3–5)	■ Language and literacy ■ Mathematics and numeracy ■ Personal development and mutual understanding ■ Physical development and movement ■ The arts
Scotland: Curriculum for Excellence (3–18)	■ Languages ■ Mathematics ■ Health and well-being ■ Sciences ■ Religious and moral education ■ Social studies ■ Technologies ■ Expressive arts

Country	Area of learning
Wales: Foundation Phase (3–7)	■ Language, literacy and communication skills ■ Mathematical development ■ Personal and social development, well-being and cultural diversity ■ Welsh language development ■ Knowledge and understanding of the world ■ Physical development ■ Creative development

Source: Standards & Testing Agency (2018), CCEA (2006), Scottish Government (2008), Welsh Government (2015)

The activities suggested in Part 2 can be adapted to suit the developmental stages and needs of different children. As individuals, children develop at different rates and they do not progress in all areas at the same time. However, there are broad developmental stages that children pass through. The guidance for the Early Years Foundation Stage in England identifies six overlapping stages from birth to five (Table 2). Within each of these there are plenty of opportunities for adults to use objects as a basis for young children's active learning.

Table 2. Examples of activities using objects linked to areas of learning and experience (0–5 years)

Phase	Examples of activities
40–60 months	■ Make 2D and 3D models using natural objects – wood, stone, rock or seaweed (CD) ■ Justify and explain why safety is important when handling certain materials (PD)

Phase	Examples of activities
30–50 months	■ Use pictures and objects to illustrate counting songs, rhymes and number stories (MD) ■ Provide areas for children to explore the properties of objects, such as a cafe, builders' yard or garden centre (KUW)
22–30 months	■ Tell stories using real objects (CLL) ■ Talk about technologies such as computers, CD-ROMs and radios (KUW)
16–26 months	■ Display and talk about pictures showing familiar objects (CLL) ■ Sort and match collections of objects (MD)
8–20 months	■ Talk about how objects are alike and how objects, such as a sponge, can change their shape by being squeezed or stretched (KUW)
0–11 months	■ Talk to babies about objects belonging to special people – for example, family members like grandparents (CLL) ■ Provide objects for babies to hold, suck, pull and squeeze (PSED)

Source: Adapted from Early Education (2012)

Key: CD – creative development, PD – physical development, MD – mathematical development, KUW – knowledge and understanding of the world, CLL – communication, language and literacy, PSED – personal, social and emotional development.

The Appendix includes a map to show how the activities align to the four skills of communication, collaboration, critical thinking and creativity, which are widely acknowledged as being important for children's long-term development.

3. Why focus on developing communication, collaboration, critical thinking and creativity?

Although objects can be used to promote a wide range of skills, we have focused on communication, collaboration, critical thinking and creativity (Figure 5). These skills are recognised internationally as essential for children and young people's development. These are also the skills that employers particularly value. The foundations for this lifelong learning begin in the early years. Research shows clearly that early childhood is a critical period in children's development and education because this is when they are most receptive to interventions that can have a lasting impact (Schweinhart et al., 2005).

Figure 5. Four key skills for children's development

In the United States, the 4 C's have been explicitly endorsed by the Partnership for 21st Century Learning (P21, 2016), a major coalition of business leaders, educationalists and policymakers established in 2002. We believe schools should focus on the 4 C's because these are central to helping children and young people succeed in life. Today's school leavers need to have the know-how to negotiate constant change, given that they are likely to work in a range of jobs. While proficiency in reading, writing and mathematics is important, this is not sufficient in the modern world. Young people also need to be competent at solving problems, collaborating and thinking critically.

The World Economic Forum's report, *New Vision for Education: Fostering Social and Emotional Learning through Technology*, highlights the gap between the skills learned in school and those needed in work and life. It recommends a range of teaching approaches to develop twenty-first century skills from an *early* age, including a hands-on approach, defined as: 'instructional strategies that involve learning by doing and thus allow the child to actively participate in an activity, typically including objects, materials and other elements' (2016: 27).

Communication

The four core skills of communication – reading, writing and, to a lesser extent, speaking and listening – have always had a strong presence in the school curriculum. However, the power of modern media and the ubiquitous nature of digital technologies in all aspects of our lives make the teaching of effective communication skills even more important. Children need to be taught how to express themselves clearly in a variety of forms and contexts. They should learn how to decipher meaning, including knowledge, values and intentions. They also need to be skilful in using multimedia platforms as a form of communication. While automation and robotics have led to the loss of many jobs, they cannot match the face-to-face people skills of persuasion, listening with empathy, reading body language, negotiating difficulties and responding sensitively. Social and emotional intelligence is wrapped up in effective communication skills. We know that young children who learn to take turns – for example, in asking questions about objects – can keep and make friends more easily (Seefeldt, 2004).

It is widely perceived that too many children are entering and leaving school without the most basic communication skills. Based on a survey of 500 teachers, the charity Save the Children reported in 2015 that 75% of children enter reception unable to speak in full sentences, while another survey suggests that more than half of business leaders are dissatisfied with school leavers' communication skills (Cassidy, 2017). Research is less conclusive on whether children's communication skills are declining, although organisations such as the National Literacy Trust (2005) are concerned enough to ask whether buggies in which babies are facing away from the adult (and therefore less likely to interact) are to blame. Undoubtedly, strong parental modelling and high quality teaching can make a significant difference in supporting children's language development.

Despite widely held support for the importance of communication skills in the school curriculum, in practice teaching does not focus enough on developing the kinds of communication that school leavers need when they enter the workplace. Over the last decade or so, Robin Alexander has written extensively on the need to spend more time on talking to learn rather than the ineffective talking for teaching which is prevalent in many classrooms. His 'dialogic classroom' (2005) has several characteristics: teachers and pupils listen to each other, share ideas and consider alternative viewpoints (reciprocal); learners are encouraged to articulate their ideas freely without fear or embarrassment (supportive); both teachers and learners build on their own and each other's ideas (cumulative); teachers plan sessions with clear learning intentions and goals in mind (purposeful); and, finally, teachers and pupils work together as co-learners (collective).

Objects can support children learning English as an additional language. They can associate objects with events or lessons: being given a spoon might signify lunchtime, a book might preface using the library or a paintbrush introduce an art lesson. Objects can be used to help children develop language, express choices and support routines, timetables and schedules. A child may not be able to say the word 'toilet', but if they point to a toilet-roll holder or show you a picture of a toilet then the message is clear.

Some children with special educational needs, such as visual impairment and autism, find things easier to understand when they can handle an object. If a child learns to attach a special meaning to an object it becomes an 'object of reference'. This is illustrated in the story of Afzal, who had no functional vision (RNIB, 2014). She often became anxious in school when it was time to go home because she didn't understand where she was being taken. However, because Afzal always held on to her seatbelt in the car, it was decided to give her a piece of seatbelt webbing immediately before going to the car. The hope was that this would help her to understand she was going in the car. Each time the webbing was presented, the person giving it to her also said, 'Afzal; car'. Within a few days, Afzal relaxed when she was given the webbing. She had attached the special meaning of 'car' to the webbing, which became an object of reference for her in supporting her understanding.

It can take much longer for other children to establish a link between the object and the place, person, event or experience it relates to, so it is important to see objects of reference as specific to each child (Ockleford, 2002). Objects can be used as location or activity markers around the classroom or school – a book placed in front of the library, a tambourine for music or some dice ahead of a mathematics session. In time, objects can be replaced with abstract symbols.

Collaboration

Although children can explore and learn about objects on their own, we want to emphasise the importance of using objects to trigger group discussion and collaboration. Interaction is an important means by which children learn about themselves and others. They learn social norms such as turn taking and respecting opinions that they may not agree with. Social learning theory (Bandura, 1976) advocates that because humans are social creatures, we learn by observing others and through a continual process of interacting with people and the environment. Increasingly, teamwork is acknowledged as a key skill in the workplace. The writer James Surowiecki (2005) points out that collective intelligence – what he terms 'the wisdom of crowds' – is far more powerful and productive than individual effort. Greater knowledge is created and shared as students work together rather than in isolation. We know that constructive (as opposed to argumentative) collaboration enables children to build ideas and develop as thinkers (Mercer, 2000).

However, working well together is challenging because children come to understand that others see and interpret the same thing in different ways from them. By the age of about four, most children develop the capacity to recognise that others will hold different feelings *and* thoughts and so see the world differently to them – what is known as a 'theory of mind'. One way of assessing whether children have a theory of mind is to tell them a story in which one character believes something the children know to be untrue, such as where an object is hidden. If the children correctly predict the character's actions in following a mistaken belief they are said to have a reasonably well-developed theory of mind (Anning and Edwards, 2006). Clearly, to get the most out of working with others, children need to reach this stage of development.

It is important, therefore, that teachers plan opportunities to observe children working together to assess how well they appreciate the perspectives of others. Children need regular opportunities to discuss objects in groups, where they can share ideas, learn to follow group rules such as listening respectfully to the views of others and taking turns, and assume responsibilities as team members. If particular group tasks are set, such as making a presentation to the rest of the class on the story behind an object, children can learn important skills about meeting group goals, working to time, giving feedback to others, offering to help others and communicating effectively.

However, children do not automatically acquire effective collaborative skills. Adults need to model these and provide children with guidance so they know what is socially acceptable. Discussion can be framed so that children begin to reason and reach informed conclusions – for example:

■ In our group discussion, we were thinking that the object is …

■ Our guess is that the object was made to …

■ We thought it was used by … because …

■ We thought something else because …

■ We agree/disagree with the other group because …

■ We are not sure whether you would agree, but we thought …

■ We did some research and found …

The research evidence suggests that effective collaborative learning is much more than just sitting pupils around a table and asking them to work together; it requires carefully designed tasks and approaches that promote purposeful talk and interaction.[1] And so, while there are times when young children should explore objects independently, teachers also need to plan for more structured adult input to enable them to develop collaborative learning habits such as listening with empathy. Children will need direct input on what it means to be a good listener. Simple checklists can be devised to remind children of what to look for – for example, one person speaks at a time, use the word 'because' to explain an answer and do not shout. In group work, individuals need to know what is expected of them, such as how they are going to work together in observing, discussing and recording the object. At times, it may prove beneficial to assign roles to each group member (e.g. observer, artist, reporter, summariser, questioner).

Critical thinking

Critical thinking involves reflecting purposefully on what we know, believe and do. We know that by the time young people reach college or university, the skills they possess in problem solving, reasoning and analysing situations are more important than the content knowledge studied in determining their success (Conley, 2007). Teaching with objects supports the development of a range of thinking skills, including comparing, contrasting, classifying, seeing relationships, determining cause and effect, formulating questions and predicting. Young children can sort objects according to different criteria (e.g. colour, size, length), play matching games (e.g. old and new) and

---

1   See https://educationendowmentfoundation.org.uk/evidence-summaries/
    teaching-learning-toolkit/collaborative-learning/.

sequence objects (e.g. according to age or popularity). The focus for this book, however, is on promoting critical thinking. This is defined as the ability to analyse, evaluate and interpret information. Children can be encouraged to think critically about what they are doing through questions such as, 'Why do you think this?' and 'How could we make this even better?'

There is clear evidence that the most effective early years practice includes what researchers call 'sustained shared thinking' (Siraj-Blatchford et al., 2002). This most commonly occurs between an adult and a child on a one-to-one basis when both are fully absorbed in a conversation or other experience. Both adult and child must be contributing to the thinking, which should carry on for at least several minutes and can take different forms – for example, asking questions (enquiry skills), gathering ideas, reasoning (forming opinions based on information gathered), evaluating information, problem solving or generating new ideas (creative thinking). Adults can model open-ended questions such as, 'Can you find another way to …?', 'What might we do here?' or 'Why do you think that happened?' Other strategies to sustain shared thinking include inviting children to elaborate ('Can you tell me a bit more about this?'), suggesting ('Why don't you try …?'), recapping ('So you think that …'), using sense-making phrases ('I agree with …', 'I imagine that …', 'I like this idea because …') and showing genuine interest (e.g. through smiling, nodding, affirming, giving whole-class attention).

Creativity

There is no doubt that creativity is much needed in a world where few problems have only one solution. Creativity has been defined as the ability to produce something new through imaginative skill (Robinson, 2009; Wright, 2010). It is not expected that a young child will create something new that is valuable to society, but rather is original in relation to their personal stage of development. In the Reggio Emilia approach to early years education, the focus is on the creative process rather than the quality of the products or outcomes because children are still developing their creative skills. Anna Craft's (2000) notion of 'possibility thinking' neatly sums up what lies at the heart of creativity – being imaginative, posing questions and playing with ideas. Every child should have the capacity to express themselves creatively. They are naturally creative – they ask questions, poke around, take things apart, play with ideas and live in imaginary worlds. They can speculate over who used objects, imagine what they may have been like in their original state and generate ideas on how the objects could be used in different ways. In history sessions, children can consider what objects tell us about change over time. In geography sessions, the focus may shift towards what objects reveal about a sense of place and culture. In religious education, objects can shed light on people's beliefs and values.

Unfortunately, research suggests that schools are not doing enough to promote children's creativity. A major study in the United States reports that since 1990, while IQ scores are rising slightly, creativity in schools has significantly declined as measured by standardised tests (Kim, 2011). The research shows that children have become less energetic, less articulate, less imaginative, less unconventional, less likely to see things from a different angle and less apt to make connections between apparently irrelevant things. The 'creativity crisis' has been attributed to the emphasis on a culture of monitoring, evaluation, tests and prescribed curricula.

It is also the case that there are many misconceptions around creativity which have not helped to move the agenda forward. These include notions that creativity is confined to the arts, is limited to a relatively small number of gifted individuals, is only for the young and is not something that you can teach or assess. In fact, we know that creativity is essential in all walks of life – science, technology, mathematics, sport, literature – and has been demonstrated by people of all ages. Picasso's most inventive work was produced in his seventies and eighties. What matters more than anything is a learning environment that supports questioning, persistence, openness to fresh ideas and tolerance of 'glorious failures'.

Good teachers for creativity pose open-ended questions, encourage collaborative group work, think aloud various possibilities, facilitate critical evaluation of ideas and promote experiment and enquiry. Children can demonstrate their creative energies by thinking about how they might improve on the objects they examine, given that one of the principles of 'knowledge building' is that all ideas are improvable. But this takes time, patience, trust and resilience. School leaders need to trust teachers to develop creativity in the classroom, without the pressures of eyeing test scores. As the Partnership for 21st Century Learning points out, creativity and innovation are long-term skills that form 'a cyclical process of small successes and frequent mistakes' (Trilling and Fadel, 2009: 59).

4. What is the theory behind using objects?

The use of objects is supported by a range of educational theories and models. Learning theories advocated by heavyweight figures such as Lev Vygotsky (1962, 1978) and Jerome Bruner (1960) emphasise that learning takes place in a social context and through discussion, where thinking is initiated, developed and modified. In short, children learn by doing, exploring and thinking. The skills associated with the handling and interpretation of objects align particularly well with discovery, experiential, enquiry-based, problem-based, project-based and real-world learning theories. These theories emphasise the importance of children asking questions about their world, searching for meaning and constructing a worldview based on dialogue, experience and first-hand observation. Knowledge is viewed as something that is co-constructed and fluid rather than fixed and transmitted by others, usually those in authority.

This book focuses on using objects to develop skills in communication, collaboration, critical thinking and creativity. One very useful model to support this is Thinking Routines, which is the work of Ron Ritchhart (2002) and colleagues from Project Zero at Harvard University (http://pz.harvard. edu). These academics set out to improve children's thinking through simple, flexible, easy-to-teach routines. One routine that works well with objects is called See, Think, Wonder (STW). It was originally created to develop children's understanding of artwork in galleries. STW focuses attention on why something looks the way it does or is the way it is. Children are encouraged to make observations about an object, image or event, answering three questions: 'What do you see?', 'What do you think about that?' and 'What does it make you wonder?'

Seeing

To begin with, children talk about what they see. In our experience, it is useful to add further structure through prompts which focus on an object's features such as:

■ What (two, three, etc.) colours can you see?

■ What types of materials can you see?

■ What kind of shape is the object?

■ What most interests you?

■ Can you see any … (e.g. numbers, words, dates, characters) on the object?

It is important to remember that this part of the routine focuses on promoting observational skills.

Thinking

The second stage involves encouraging children to think about the object and to justify what they say with evidence derived from what they can see. This can be structured through the prompts mentioned in Figure 6. Children can be arranged in pairs as 'talk partners' or 'listening triangles' to share ideas and express likes and dislikes. With the latter, children take on the role of speaker (who explains the topic), questioner (who finds areas to clarify further) and note-taker (who observes).

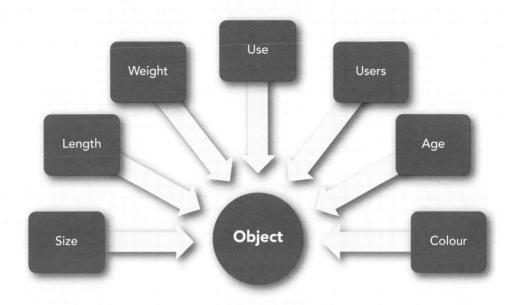

Figure 6. Features of objects

We have found that a useful phrase to model for young children is, 'I think … because …'

Wondering

The third stage involves children comparing what they are finding out about an object with their existing knowledge. The idea is to promote questioning and further enquiry. Adults can model this by thinking aloud using phrases such as:

◾ I wonder who … (might use/have used this)?

◾ I wonder when this was made?

◾ I wonder why this was made?

◾ I wonder what this object would tell us about its life if it could talk?

■ I wonder where I can find out more about this?

■ Imagine if this was a different (colour, size, shape, etc.) …

5. What is the role of the teacher?

Over the years, much discussion about teaching styles has been reduced to two basic approaches. Teachers are either seen as employing a didactic approach, in which they transmit knowledge and tell children what to do, or they are cast as facilitators, where they encourage children to take an active role in lessons. The latter is particularly associated with early years practice, where an exploratory approach is said to deepen children's understanding and disposition to learn further (Eaude, 2012).

In object-based learning, the teacher can adopt a different role along a continuum depending on the extent to which children take the lead in the learning. At one end of the continuum, children can be given objects to explore without any prompts as part of imaginative or free play. At the other end of the continuum, objects are used by teachers as resources to illustrate teaching points in more traditional lessons characterised by direct instruction. In most Early Years Foundation Stage classrooms children have regular opportunities to play with objects independently or in small groups. There are times when teachers may opt to leave an object out on a table without any explanation to incite curiosity, perhaps as a starting point for a topic. A teacher may also use objects as focal points for teaching specific skills, such as observing, sketching or comparing.

In using the objects outlined in Part 2, we see the teacher as seeking to enthuse, engage and challenge learners. One of this book's aims is to provide teachers with a clear understanding of how objects can be used to promote effective learning. Over the years, there has been much discussion (and confusion) about the differences between aims, goals, learning objectives, desirable outcomes, intended learning outcomes and learning intentions, to mention just some of the most popular terms. Presently, the

Early Years Foundation Stage in England uses the term 'early learning goals', whereas 'foundation phase outcomes' is the preferred term in Welsh schools, describing 'the type and range of achievements characteristic of children within the Foundation Phase (3–7)' (Welsh Government, 2015: 49). In Northern Ireland's Foundation Stage, official guidance refers to the use of 'learning intentions' (CCEA, 2007: 11), while Scotland's Curriculum for Excellence features 'experiences and outcomes' defined as 'clear and concise statements about children's learning and progression in each curriculum area'.[2]

For convenience, we have simplified this in Part 2 by including examples of learning goals/intentions related to suggested activities for practitioners to reflect upon. Essentially, what matters is that teachers have a clear idea about their role and what they will do and what children should experience (e.g. playing and exploring) and learn (e.g. to follow instructions) through the course of using the objects.

To enthuse

We learn best when we are motivated to learn and are interested in the topic. Enthusiasm means having an intense interest in something and showing an eagerness to learn more. Enthusiastic learners and teachers are easy to spot: they are animated, energetic and usually mobile. Classroom observers can quickly pick up verbal and non-verbal signs of teacher enthusiasm, such as the selection and delivery of words, eye contact, facial expressions, gestures and energy level. One academic considered the level of enthusiasm as the distinguishing feature between good and great teachers and developed what she called an Enthusiasm Awareness Index to support teachers in their journey (Sanders, 1985). At the high end this includes teachers (and learners) who maintain excellent eye contact (while avoiding staring); use frequent changes of expression; make highly descriptive word choices; perform quick and demonstrative gestures; make vibrant facial expressions; have highly varied tone, pitch, volume and cadence; and express general exuberance.

2   See https://education.gov.scot/scottish-education-system/policy-for-scottish-education/ policy-drivers/cfe-(building-from-the-statement-appendix-incl-btc1-5)/Experiences%20 and%20outcomes.

The challenge for practitioners is to demonstrate and instil enthusiasm. The most effective teachers are the enthusiastic ones (Stronge et al., 2004; Coe et al., 2014). Classroom observations of the most enthusiastic teachers show that those teachers who show a general enthusiasm for teaching are more effective than those who are passionate about their particular subjects. Clearly, what matters is having what Shulman (1987) called 'pedagogical content knowledge', which describes how skilful teachers bring together knowledge of how and what to teach so they can create effective learning environments.

To engage

The term 'engagement' is often used in education to describe the curiosity, effort and persistence demonstrated by learners. It matters because research tells us that there is a strong correlation between high levels of engagement and improved achievement and attendance (Willingham et al., 2002). It is not difficult to see when young children are engaged in their learning. Observing a young child carefully touch a spider's web in the school grounds and watch open mouthed as the spider crawls out – and then do the same thing else-where for the fifth time – is seeing engagement at its best. Practitioner guidance for the Early Years Foundation Stage points out that play, in all its forms, requires active engagement and can be deeply satisfying (DCSF, 2009). Practitioners provide engaging learning experiences when they allow children to investigate, share, make choices, nurture creative thinking, play games and build on what they already know. Popular strategies include:

■ Posing questions and open-ended challenges – e.g. 'How many ways can you sort …?'

■ Quick games – e.g. 'I'm thinking of a number' or 'twenty questions'.

■ Think–pair–share – children briefly talk to a partner about a particular question or topic and then share ideas back to the whole group.

■ Dramatic techniques – e.g. role play, hot seating, freeze-frame.

Building on the early work of Bloom et al. (1956), research on learner engagement describes different dimensions (Brewster and Fager, 2000; Marks, 2000). Children who are *behaviourally* engaged comply with social norms such as attendance and participation, and do not prove disruptive. Children who engage *emotionally* react with interest, enjoyment and a sense of belonging. Finally, children who are *cognitively* engaged relish learning and respond to the challenges presented, such as solving problems. Disengaged learners are those who are apathetic, bored or withdrawn. Schlechty (2011) suggests that there are five levels of engagement (Figure 7). At the lowest 'rebellion' level there are students who refuse to do assigned tasks and act disruptively, and next there are those who retreat by not participating in the activity. At both these levels the students learn very little, if anything. The third level of engagement is characterised by students going through the ritual of learning, but they are only interested in avoiding negative consequences such as being reprimanded for not staying on task. At the fourth level of strategic compliance, learning happens but it is motivated by the desire to attain a particular reward. Finally, deep engagement occurs when students are highly committed to complete a task because they see its inherent value and meaning to them. They persist at what they are doing, even though this may prove challenging.

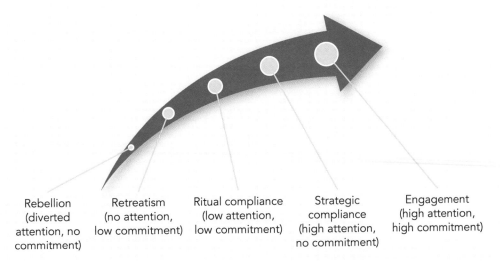

Rebellion (diverted attention, no commitment)

Retreatism (no attention, low commitment)

Ritual compliance (low attention, low commitment)

Strategic compliance (high attention, no commitment)

Engagement (high attention, high commitment)

Figure 7. Levels of engagement

Source: Based on Schlechty (2011)

Engagement begins by capturing children's interest in the content, and, in this book, we argue that objects are an excellent means of doing this. It also requires practitioners to elicit responses from the children using questions and prompts. Children also need feedback on their engagement. Effective facilitation is the key to engagement. This means striking the right balance between input from adults and the learners.

To challenge

The literature on extending young children's thinking suggests that this typically falls into four phases (Walsh et al., 2010). We have adapted these to show how objects can be used (Figure 8).

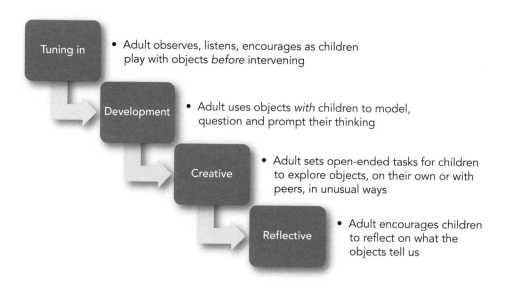

Figure 8. Stages in extending children's thinking using objects

Source: Based on Walsh et al. (2010)

At the *tuning in* stage, adults leave children to explore independently objects of their choice. They might investigate natural objects in the school grounds such as logs or leaves, pebbles on the beach or puddles in the playground. The role of the adult is to observe, take careful notes and encourage exploratory play. The *development* stage involves adults using the objects to raise questions or model thinking aloud. For instance, they might pose some puzzles: 'I wonder how the stones get in the puddle?', 'How can we find out how deep it is?', 'Why does the water turn brown?', 'What happened to the water yesterday?' At the *creative* stage, adults set open-ended tasks to encourage the children's imagination, so they can think beyond the usual routines, using prompts such as, 'I wonder what might happen if ...?', 'Are there other ways to do this?' This is about supporting children to move from black-and-white to possibility or divergent thinking. The highest state of challenge occurs when children demonstrate metacognitive behaviour and *reflective* thinking – they plan what they want to do (how and when), they ask themselves questions, review their learning and that of others, suggesting what they might do differently and why. Practitioners can extend children's thinking through various strategies, including introducing new words and new ideas, modelling more complex ways of speaking, thinking out loud, posing new problems, encouraging negotiation of conflicts, explaining or demonstrating approaches.

We are suggesting that adults use their professional judgement to decide when to observe children playing with objects, when to use the objects as visual resources for teaching points and when to set object-related tasks. The most effective teachers use a range of approaches to suit the subject being taught, the children's age and stage of development, the mood of the class and, above all, what the teacher is trying to achieve. The key point with object-based learning, as with all pedagogies, is to align lesson aims with activities and suitable resources. There is no point aiming to develop children's communication skills, such as speaking and listening, and then ignoring children's comments that you are not giving them enough time to talk about objects.

We know that expert teachers value the importance of modelling. Several writers (e.g. Rogoff, 1991) support the apprenticeship approach to teaching, where children learn from observing and practising alongside adults who model the desired learning outcomes, such as how to interact with others, how to approach a task or particular qualities such as persistence. Clearly, children need good role models but this should not leave them with the impression that teachers are all-knowing. Part of the modelling should include handling uncertainty and having the confidence to have a go. Teachers need to show curiosity in the world around them, demonstrate an open-minded attitude and display an eagerness to learn.

Teachers cannot expect children to be creative if the environment does not support this. Children need to feel psychologically safe to suggest ideas, make mistakes and take risks. It is the responsibility of teachers to build relationships so that children give and receive criticism in the right spirit. They should provide tools, resources and experiences that enable learners to explore, reflect and discuss possible questions that they pose about objects. For example, they might be asked to improve upon an object by changing one aspect (e.g. making it smaller or bigger, adding or removing a part, changing a colour).

What matters here is the creative thinking process rather than the actual outcome. Children need the confidence to look at an object in a fluid rather than fixed way, to consider different uses and users and to imagine what might happen if the object was modified in some way or another. In short, teachers should introduce young children to the world of designers and use real-life examples to illustrate how these techniques are applied. For instance, consider the example of the ballpoint pen; it's possible to buy mini pens for key rings, pens with multiple coloured inks, gold-plated luxury pens, pens which double as pencils or tools such as screwdrivers and torches and so forth.

To ask questions

One of the key roles of the teacher in object-based enquiry is to ask well-conceived questions and encourage pupils to do so themselves. These questions can be a blend of closed and open-ended types, designed to elicit information about the object and the wider context. One simple thing to bear in mind when devising questions is to consider using the journalistic technique of the Five W's (and one H), each beginning with an interrogative word: Who? What? Where? When? Why? and How? Journalists use this approach when seeking to gain comprehensive information. Usually, the questions stimulate more than a 'yes' or 'no' answer. These stems can form the basis of the following questions:

- Who uses/might have used the object (e.g. children, adults, elderly people, mums)?

- What is the object made of?

- What is it for?

- Where might the object be used (e.g. at home, in an office, outside)?

- When might this object be used (e.g. time of day, season, year)?

- Why is the object this colour/shape/size?

- How do you think it is/was made?

Table 3 gives examples of more detailed questions that can be asked when using objects. It is based on the taxonomy of educational objectives originally drawn up by Bloom et al. (1956) and revised by Anderson and Krathwohl (2001).

Table 3. Questions to ask in relation to objects based on revised Bloom's taxonomy

Level	Key words	Question stems
Remember	Define, label, name, recall, list, identify, spell, tell	■ What colour, shape, etc. is this object? ■ Where could it have been used? ■ Can you write a label for this object? ■ Who uses it/might have used it? When? ■ How? How much? How many?

Level	Key words	Question stems
Understand	Put in your own words, explain, describe, sequence	■ What does this mean? ■ What can we say for certain (facts) about this object? ■ Can you describe the object to another person without looking at it? ■ Can you explain to someone ...? ■ Why is the object important? ■ To whom might the object be important?
Apply	Give an example, make, show, draw, construct, find out, put into practice, use	■ Can you think of examples where/ how you could use this object? ■ Could you use the information to make a museum of objects?
Analyse	Compare, classify, contrast, examine, dissect, take apart, investigate	■ How is this object like/unlike another? ■ Can we take the object apart? What does each part do? ■ Would it work without this part? Why?
Evaluate	Choose, decide, defend, judge, rate, value, assess, justify, discuss, value, recommend, assess	■ Do you agree with ...? Why? ■ What do you think about ...? ■ Which object do you think is better/ more important? Why? ■ How do you think this ... has affected people? ■ How could the object be improved?

Level	Key words	Question stems
Create	Invent, design, change, improve, add to, compose, plan, predict, imagine	■ Do you think this is a well-designed object? ■ Can you improve the design of this one? ■ What if this object didn't exist? What difference would this make? ■ What would happen if we made this object bigger/smaller/longer/shorter? ■ What if we changed another feature (e.g. colour)? ■ Can you adapt the object for a new audience? ■ Can you design your own object?

Teachers need to ask questions to increase the level of challenge in lessons. Initially, questions can be asked to keep the flow of learning, to engage all and to check what children have understood. Questions can then progress by seeking to draw out the children's opinions and ideas, to create a sense of shared learning and to direct questions at particular learners. Finally, questions can encourage higher level thinking such as generating ideas (e.g. 'How many different uses of this object can you think of?') and foster speculation (e.g. 'What if we no longer had this object?').

6. How do I create an object-rich environment?

The richness of the learning environment can make an important contribution to children's creativity (Vecchi, 2010). In the 1970s, the architect Simon Nicholson developed the theory of loose parts in which he suggested that creativity follows when the environment is designed to be fluid rather than static. This theory provides a basis to create an inspiring play-based environment for young children (Beloglovsky et al., 2016). Being creative is usually a messy process, and so materials need to be on hand for young children to express their ideas – from dressing-up clothes to using pots, pans and spoons as musical instruments.

Both the indoor and outdoor learning environments should contain stimulating and vibrant resources. For instance, objects relating to the seasons should be made readily available for children to handle and explore. A rainy day box might include umbrellas, waterproof jackets, toy boats, containers for collecting water and tapes to measure the sizes of puddles. Objects for windy days might include streamers, chimes, windmills and kites, whereas magnifying glasses, sandals and sun cream would support learning on sunny days. Collections of objects can be grouped around the elements:

- **Fire**: cardboard boxes, logs, mirrors, paper, small world figures, twigs, tools, wood offcuts

- **Air**: feathers, ferns, kites, leaves, masks, fabrics, tubes

- **Water**: small boats, bowls, corks, shells, spades, buckets, buoys, sieves, umbrellas, yoghurt pots, saucepans, paper cups, sponges, mop and bucket, balloon whisks, balls, washboard, trays, rubber gloves, small fishing nets, objects for bridges, plastic fish, rocks, plastic ducks, pipes

- **Earth**: buckets, cartons, cones, conkers, custard powder tins, egg cups, funnels, ladles, plastic cups, diggers, bottles, natural materials, plastic bags, plastic flowers, wheelbarrow

In preparing the learning environment, teachers should ensure that there is a strong emphasis on providing sensory experiences. Children learn and remember more effectively when play involves touching, smelling, hearing, tasting and seeing. They need to work with objects and materials that can easily be moved around.

Although children are naturally inclined to move objects, they can also learn a lot without necessarily touching them. It is worth discussing with children why it may not be appropriate to handle an object – perhaps it is too fragile, too precious or too dangerous. In museums, some objects are so valuable (e.g. due to their age, rareness or beauty) they are not even exhibited. Children can learn by sketching the objects, relating them to their own experience or listening to associated stories.

Some young children may not be able to pick up and manipulate objects for themselves. However, objects can be hung down around them for them to look at, touch and listen to. It is important to consider where to place sensory objects in relation to the child – for example, some children find it easier to reach in front of them, whereas others prefer to reach to one side. Find out each child's visual range and use objects within this limit.

7. Where can I find the objects?

All of the objects featured in Part 2 can be found around the school, at home, in local shops and in the immediate environment. Since the 1990s 'Discount Britain' has emerged with the growth of bargain shops on the high street – 99p Stores, Poundland, Home Bargains – all of which offer cheap resources for practitioners. Antique fairs, flea markets and second-hand shops offer another source – for example, old work tools that are not commonly used today can stimulate much discussion. The natural environment is a good starting point for collecting objects: gardens, parks, woodlands (e.g. leaves, moss, feathers), hedgerows (e.g. twigs, old nests), beaches (e.g. seashells, pebbles), hills and mountains (e.g. rocks). Clear bags and rubber gloves can be used to collect natural, organic objects, which should be washed before use or they can be handled in tightly sealed plastic bags. The plastic bag prevents oils on the children's hands from being transferred onto the objects. Mothballs can be placed inside bags to stop insects from destroying the collection.

The skills that we refer to can be developed with less mundane objects held in museums, galleries and other public spaces. Over the past twenty or so years, museums have increasingly explored ways of making their collections accessible to young children. Education officers have worked on the notion that children should make their own meaning by interacting with exhibits. Most of the national museums have produced excellent resources to support practitioners in using their collections. The British Museum, for example, has a scheme in which 100 objects are selected across time periods, places and themes to inspire children (www.teachinghistory100.org). These include a domestic object, a bucket, from the time of the Great Fire of London in 1666. The leather bears the initials 'SBB' and traces of the first three figures of the date painted on it (166 – the final digit is unclear), but the bucket may have been dropped during the chaos of the Great Fire. It was not discovered until 1974, found in a burned out cellar at the end of Pudding Lane. The objects have accompanying teachers' notes and lesson ideas.

GEM, an organisation dedicated to heritage learning, includes guidance for teachers on techniques for using objects to satisfy children's innate curiosity and desire to touch (www.gem.org.uk). The National Museum of Ireland's website advocates an enquiry-based, dialogical approach to examining artefacts. Using Bronze Age artefacts as a context, it includes guidance for teachers on asking questions, facilitating discussion, using concept maps, stories, dilemmas and enquiry frames (http://microsites.museum.ie/ bronzeagehandlingbox/teachers-strategies.html). Many of these ideas can be adapted for teaching through everyday objects. Visitors to museums are often engaged by the stories that accompany objects. The use of reconstructed scenes, immersive displays and dioramas are important in helping visitors to make sense of objects in context, specifically how, where and when something was used. The Canadian-based Let's Talk Science projects (http:// letstalkscience.ca) enable children to appreciate the science associated with everyday objects. Jopson (2015) describes why teapots dribble, toast burns and light bulbs shine.

Part 2

A–Z of everyday objects

A is for Apples

In a nutshell

Apples originated in China and there is evidence that they grew wild in prehistoric Britain. However, the Romans introduced sweeter apples and King Alfred was the first recorded person to have eaten an apple in about 885 AD. The Normans brought us French apples and monks cultivated fine orchards. In the nineteenth century, farmers experimented with pollination methods to produce now famous eating apples such as Cox's Orange Pippin. Today, there are many varieties and sizes, from those slightly larger than a cherry to one bigger than a grapefruit.

A 2011 poll in *The Telegraph* found that Britain's favourite top three apples are: Gala, Cox and Braeburn. Leading chef Raymond Blanc suggests that Britons choose the sweeter Gala over Cox because many are addicted to sugar – some apples sold in supermarkets contain 12% sugar.

However, the saying 'an apple a day keeps the doctor away' seems to be true. Apples contain no fat, sodium or cholesterol and are a good source of fibre. They help to lower blood fats. A paper published in the journal *Appetite* suggests that eating a medium-sized apple fifteen minutes before a meal can reduce your calorific intake by an average of 15%, which equates to about sixty more calories than contained in the apple. There are many organisations that promote healthy eating among school-children – for example, the Soil Association's Food for Life, the Children's Food Trust and Food in Schools.

Today, an Internet search for 'apple' is more likely to provide information on computers rather than fruit, such is the global success of Apple's Macintosh computers.

Did you know?

■ Apple trees take four to five years to produce their first fruit.

■ Apples ripen six to ten times faster at room temperature than if they are refrigerated.

■ More than 50% of apples in the world are harvested in China.

■ Britons eat 80% more red apples than green ones.

■ New York City is called 'The Big Apple'. The saying comes from the 1920s, when horseracing was popular and the prizes were apples. A journalist used the phrase after hearing stable hands say they were going to 'The Big Apple' to work at the event.

■ People who sold apples in the Middle Ages were called 'costardmongers' – a Costard was a variety of apple and the word 'monger' means trader.

■ The Apple computer name came from the owner Steve Jobs who had visited an apple farm as part of a diet. The famous logo created in 1977, which features a bite out of an apple, was included for scale so people did not think it was a cherry.

Ready

- **Key resources**: variety of apples, knife and plate, world map (Activity 1); coloured card and tissue, glue, glue sticks, saucers, scissors (Activity 2); collection of recipes (Activity 3); colour charts, apples (Activity 4).

- **Health and safety**: washing hands before and after cooking and after visiting garden/allotments, suitable footwear/clothing when visiting.

- **Key vocabulary**: seed, sapling, fruit, shoot, water, sunlight, fertiliser, orchard, blossom, pollination, picking, storing, eating, explain.

Steady

Before teaching, reflect on the following goals/learning intentions:

- To understand where apples come from and how apples are produced.

- To know that fruit is an important part of a healthy diet.

- To identify different varieties of apples with different characteristics.

Go

Use examples of apples and other food to discuss with children their ideas of where they think apples come from before they arrive on the shelves of shops or supermarkets. Refer to a world map if necessary. Where did their journey begin?

Activity 1: Apple tasting

Chop the apples into small segments and blindfold 'tasters' so the children can describe the taste of each one. Which is their favourite? How do the tastes differ? Encourage them to use adventurous vocabulary. Get the children to look closely at and compare different types of apple. They could create a bar chart to show their preferences and discuss these. What questions can they ask about the data?

Activity 2: Make apple art

Explore famous still life paintings that include fruit, inviting the children to talk about what they like or dislike about the painting, and looking at the techniques the artist has used. Give the children coloured tissue paper to create apples or an apple tree in the style of different artists. Encourage the children to create their own art in the style of artists such as Cézanne. Older children might make apple sculptures such as swans – show the class videos from real chefs, such as: https://www.youtube.com/watch?v=uLXEiMIiF5E.

Activity 3: Cook with apples

Follow some simple recipes featuring apples – for some ideas see: https://www.bbcgoodfood.com/recipes/collection/apple. Make instructional videos to show others how to cook apple crumble, for example. Make fun healthy snacks using crackers, pretzel sticks and apple slices. What would be an ideal healthy lunchbox?

Activity 4: Visit an allotment, orchard or garden

Give the children colour charts to see if they can find an apple to match each colour or one apple that has all the colours. Get the children to explore the different ways apple trees can be grown or trained to produce more fruit that is accessible. They could also look at other fruit being grown in the garden, and if permission is granted, pick one or two varieties to try off the tree. How do they taste compared to supermarket apples? Discuss why winter is important for apple trees even though they are bare.

Other ideas

- Explore harvests around the world – for example, Thanksgiving in the United States, the rice harvest in Indonesia and Sukkot in Israel.

- Design scarecrows: visit the Royal Horticultural Society website (www.rhs.org.uk) for instructions.

- Make apple patterns: use apples and other fruit and vegetables for printing patterns.

- Create a marketing campaign for a new British apple (fruit, not computer!).

Find out more

- The Royal Horticultural Society has lesson plans using apples at Key Stage 1: https://www.rhs.org.uk/Education-Learning/PDF/School-visits/Rosemoor/Lesson-plans/Key-stage-1/Apples-during.

- Morrisons supermarket also has examples of lesson plans using apples: http://your.morrisons.com/Documents/LetsGrow/Key%20Stage%201%20-%20Lesson%20Plans.pdf.

- The National Fruit Show has produced various resources including a guide to a year in the life of an apple tree: http://www.nationalfruitshow.org.uk/education.

- Research the role of beneficial insects in farming (e.g. lady beetles (or ladybirds) which eat spider mites; bees and hoverflies which pollinate crops) and those insects which destroy crops (e.g. whiteflies).

B is for Bubbles

In a nutshell

A bubble is simply air wrapped in a film of soap. The film is made from soap and water or other liquids. The thin layer of water is caught between two layers of soap molecules, likened to slices of bread in a water sandwich holding the air inside. Blowing bubbles with normal water doesn't work as well because the water's surface tension (the forces holding the molecules of a liquid together) is too high.

Bubble blowing has long been enjoyed as a popular pastime. Even poor families could find a wire to twist into a circle and some soap for blowing bubbles.

The eighteenth century French painter Jean-Baptiste-Siméon Chardin's *Soap Bubbles* shows a boy blowing bubbles using a bubble pipe. In 1886, a famous advertising campaign for the soap company A. & F. Pears featured a child playing with bubbles. The painting was the work of Sir John Everett Millais and the subject was his five-year-old grandson.

Around the same time, a handbook for the Boy Scouts of America devoted a chapter to blowing bubbles.

By the 1920s, the first mass produced bubble pipes and wands were available. Battery-operated bubble blowers appeared in the 1950s. Television adverts associated with soap products helped to boost sales further.

Did you know?

■ The song 'I'm Forever Blowing Bubbles' has been heard among West Ham football club supporters since the 1920s.

■ In 2003, it was reported that a Taiwanese inventor had created 'Catch-a-Bubble', a product which produces bubbles that last for ten days without popping, using a top secret polymer which resists evaporation.

■ In 2010, a record was set for the most people popping bubble wrap at one time – 1,456 people at the State Fair Meadowlands in the United States popped bubble wrap at once.

■ Gary Pearlham created the largest free-floating soap bubble in Ohio in 2015 (834 cubic feet).

■ In 2016, Stefano Righi entered the record books when he blew 730 soap bubbles by hand in one minute.

■ The British scientist Sir James Dewar kept a bubble of 32 cm diameter for 108 days.

Ready

- **Key resources**: bubble blowers/wands, straws, pipe cleaners, dishes and saucers. Bubbles are often short lived so use tablets or digital cameras to capture key moments and replay them later.

- **Health and safety**: provide goggles when young children mix and play with soapy solutions.

- **Blowing bubbles takes control**: get the children to practise breathing gently, fast, hard and so on by using a straw to blow a table tennis ball around a modelling clay maze.

- **Key vocabulary**: soap, air, big/small, round, blow, evaporate, pop, liquid, wet/dry, mixture.

Steady

What makes the best bubble mixture? To create good bubbles, you need the right recipe. The ingredients you will need are distilled water, washing-up liquid and glycerine. The Science Museum recommends mixing these in the following proportion: 95% water, 3% washing-up liquid and 2% glycerine, but the children could experiment to find a recipe that works really well. Why will this work? Adding soap lowers the surface tension of the water allowing bubbles to form, and glycerine acts to stop the bubbles drying out. They could also try making lots of bubbles at the same time by using hand whisks.

Before teaching, reflect on the following goals/learning intentions:

- To make careful observations.

- To ask questions and make predictions based on observations.

- To develop fine motor skills.

- To provide opportunities for awe and wonder.

- To use increasingly adventurous and accurate vocabulary to describe objects and events.

Go

Activity 1: Don't pop me!

Blow a bubble using a straw dipped into the mixture on a plastic saucer or similar shallow dish. Gently touch it with a pencil, pair of scissors or another pointy object. What happens? (It will pop.) Allow the children to blow bubbles and see if they can gently touch them without popping them. Blow another bubble, but this time dip the pointy object into the bubble mixture first and ask the children to predict what will happen when it touches the bubble. (This time it should not pop.) When something with bubble mixture on it touches a bubble, it doesn't make a hole in the wall of the bubble; it just slides through and the bubble re-forms right around it. See whether the children can hold a bubble in a dry hand or a soapy hand – what is the difference?

Activity 2: Try to make me a square

Ask the children to use pipe cleaners to form different shaped bubble wands (this will develop their fine motor skills) and then practise their vocabulary skills by naming these shapes. Can they blow a square bubble? A star-shaped bubble? A triangular bubble? No matter what the shape of the wand, once bubbles float into the air they are round. The skin of soap always tries to take up the least amount of space it can and round shapes take up less space. However, you can make different sized bubbles. Make big, medium and small wands, and get the children to blow hard and soft to see the difference in the bubbles they create.

Activity 3: A bubble in a bubble in a bubble

Ask the children to blow a medium-sized bubble using a medium-sized bubble wand, then quickly dip a bigger bubble wand into the bubble mix and sweep it through the air while trying to catch their little bubble inside it. With a bit of practice it is possible to catch a bubble in a bubble. Can they catch more than one? How many can they catch in thirty seconds? Or get them to blow a bubble onto a plastic lid/tray using a straw. Dip the straw into the bubble mix and very gently poke it through the bubble and try to blow a smaller bubble inside it (they should put the straw on the tray before they blow). Can they repeat this? Look at the bubble domes they have created and talk about them – what do they remind the children of? Can they describe them? How long do they last?

Activity 4: Bubble caterpillars

To make a bubble caterpillar the children will need bubble mix, a bubble wand and a straw. Invite them to blow a single bubble, catch it on the wand and hold it upside down. Dip the straw into the bubble mix and use it to blow a bubble underneath the previous bubble. Keep adding bubbles to create a caterpillar. Can they make a caterpillar of three or more bubbles? What is the longest caterpillar they can create? Can they make a caterpillar with the same number of bubbles as their friend's? Can they make mini and giant caterpillars with the same number of bubbles?

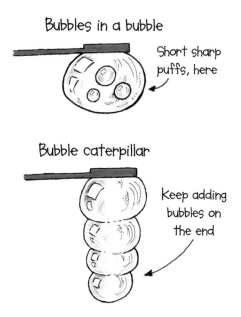

Bubbles in a bubble

Short sharp puffs, here

Bubble caterpillar

Keep adding bubbles on the end

Other ideas

- **Use dry ice to create bubbling potions**: dry ice (available from several retailers) is ideal for creating a dramatic atmosphere during story-telling. Make sure gloves are worn when handling dry ice.

- **Experiment with glowing bubbles**: use washable glowing paint (available from many online suppliers) and add that to the bubble solution (50:50). Expose the solution to a bright light for several minutes. The bubbles should then glow in the dark for that extra 'wow' factor.

- **Create colourful bubble print pictures**: add powder paint to bubble mixture (make it as thick as possible). Use a straw to blow into the mixture, and when bubbles have formed gently touch a piece of paper to them to capture the patterns formed. Use two or three colours (don't mix them together) to create colourful pictures. Look closely at the shapes and structures that are captured on the paper and talk about them.

■ **Experiment with different objects as bubble blowers**: for example, string tied in a loop, a biscuit cutter, a paperclip or soap flakes instead of bubble mix. What works best? Are any not very useful?

■ **Mark making**: bubbles and foam are an ideal sensory material for practising mark making, using fingers as well as different materials.

Find out more

■ To find out more about amazing bubble records see: http://www. guinnessworldrecords.com/world-records/ largest-free-floating-soap-bubble.

■ To find out more about bubbles and bubble products see: https://www. bubbleinc.co.uk.

■ For awe and wonder, watch a video showing a bubble artist in action – for example: https://www.youtube.com/watch?v=wdCiybJeP2w or https://www.youtube.com/watch?v=ZgttL2IGclQ.

C is for Cardboard Boxes

In a nutshell

Cardboard is essentially a heavy type of rigid and durable paper. The ancient Chinese used the earliest forms when they experimented with sheets of treated mulberry tree bark to wrap and preserve foods. In England, the first cardboard boxes were produced in 1817, and in 1890 Robert Gair invented the first pre-cut cardboard or paperboard box. This presented the retailer or shopkeeper with flat pieces which could be quickly assembled into boxes.

The first cereal boxes were created by the Kellogg's company in the 1900s, which started a revolution in food packaging. Cardboard boxes began to replace wooden crates. In recent times the question of packaging has become a major point of environmental debate. In 2010, Kellogg's had a public row with Sainsbury's, who planned to replace cardboard boxes with plastic bags for their own 'Basics' brand of cereals to reduce wastage. Kellogg's argued that their box and thin bag are fully recyclable, while thicker bags use more plastic and are harder to recycle.

Children often enjoy playing with and inside large boxes. This has led to the common cliché that, if presented with a large and expensive toy, a child will quickly become bored with the toy and play with the box instead. Although this is not necessarily the case, it is certainly true that children enjoy playing with boxes.

Did you know?

- In the UK alone, we use around 5 billion corrugated cardboard boxes each year. That is equivalent to eighty-three boxes per person!

- In 2004, the Australian architect Peter Ryan designed and built a house from cardboard boxes.

- In 2005, a cardboard box was added to the National Toy Hall of Fame in the United States.

- In France, there is a museum dedicated to cardboard and printing which features boxes used to transport silk worms.

- The online retailer Amazon uses around 1.6 million cardboard boxes every day.

- In 2016, the largest cardboard box in the world was made measuring 40 metres by 20 metres.

- Japanese artist Monami Ohno has created amazing 3D sculptures out of old cardboard boxes, including tanks, cars and spaceships.

Ready

- **Key resources**: a range of different sized boxes – parents and supermarkets are obvious sources; packaging tape and scissors (Activities 1–3); magazine pictures of cars (Activity 4).

- **Health and safety**: ensure there are no loose staples in used boxes; remind the children about the safe use of scissors.

- **Key vocabulary**: box, cardboard, small/large, smaller/larger, inside/outside, empty/full, light/heavy, corrugated, packaging, recycle, engineer, design, nets.

Steady

Before teaching, reflect on the following goals/learning intentions:

- To investigate objects and materials using different senses.

- To ask questions about how things work.

- To build a range of objects, selecting tools and techniques as appropriate.

- To share and take turns when working as a team.

Go

Activity 1: Which box next?

Gather several different sized boxes. Cover these so that they all look the same in every way except for their size. Ask the children to sort them out and then discuss how they did this. Extend the activity by, for example, adding two boxes of the same size. Next add weights into the boxes and ask the children to order them – can they predict in advance which will be heaviest or lightest? Add challenge by making small boxes heavy and large boxes light. Alternatively, leave the boxes with one open side so the children can put one box inside the other inside the other – like stacking dolls. Ask them to predict which box will fit inside which box, and model language such as 'larger', 'smaller', 'inside' and 'full'.

Activity 2: Packing parcels

Select a variety of different boxes and some wrapping paper (this could be designed by the children – e.g. printed patterns). The children can choose the box they like best and then wrap it with paper. This will develop their fine motor skills; it will involve cutting, measuring and sticking but should also encourage them to talk about the shape, size and properties of the boxes. They will need to estimate the amount of paper needed and practise mark making by drawing around the sides to create a template on the wrapping paper. This could be extended to decorate boxes for specific purposes – for example, designing and making an under the sea box, a box for a special friend or a treasure chest for pirates.

Activity 3: Deconstruction engineer

Collect a variety of boxes of different shapes and sizes and encourage the children to talk about and describe their properties. What is used to join the sides? Record images of the boxes by drawing or using digital technology. Next, undo the flaps/joins and flatten the boxes to form nets. Encourage them to talk about the shapes they can now see and explore how each different box fitted together. Can they identify straight sides, corners, edges and name the shapes they see? Can they return the box back to its original shape? Can they match the flattened boxes to the images of the original boxes – how do they know? If you collect a range of boxes with lids, the children can try to match the box to the lid, explaining how they solve the problem and using vocabulary linked to size and shape.

Activity 4: Drive-in movie

Very large boxes can be turned into all sorts of vehicles. Creating individual cars out of large boxes allows creative thought as well as mark making for a purpose (e.g. carry out a survey of registration plates in the school car park before making your own) and motor skill development. Get the children to look closely at cars and provide plenty of magazines, images, etc. to stimulate thought. They should work with a partner to plan a vehicle and decide on colours, design features and joining techniques. Provide materials to assist the making of lights, wheels, seats and so on, before holding a drive-in movie (or cartoon) experience – complete with popcorn and rows of children seated in their cardboard cars.

Other ideas

■ **Create treasure boxes for exploring natural objects through the senses**: create story boxes for small-world play, props in role play areas (e.g. a shoe shop), weather boxes, puppet theatres, robots, fortresses and dens.

■ **Play 'fill it'**: give each child a small cardboard box of the same size, then get them to take it in turns to roll a dice and then add that number of cups of sand to the box. Who will fill their box first? How many cups of sand do they predict they will need?

■ **Create a mini golf course out of cardboard boxes**: this will develop an understanding of the properties of materials as well as problem solving, creative thought and motor skill development. There are lots of opportunities to label holes; keep score; research ramps, tunnels, bridges and corners; and play a game with rules.

■ **Collect small cereal boxes and label with numbers and letters of the alphabet**: arrange these appropriately and encourage the children to fill them with the correct number of objects beginning with that letter to create a practical display.

■ **Extend early literacy skills by creating poems in a matchbox**: cut up some very simple poems or rhymes and place the words in a matchbox or similar tiny box. Allow the children to rearrange these to create their own poems – exploring rhyme, pattern and vocabulary – before performing their poem to their peers.

Find out more

■ Find poems for inspiration at: https://www.tes.com/teaching-resource/ the-poetry-station-online-poetry-video-library-6068550.

■ Use Pinterest to show children examples of artists who have created sculptures using cardboard boxes: https://www.pinterest.co.uk/explore/ cardboard-sculpture/?lp=true.

D is for Digital Cameras and Digital Photographs

In a nutshell

The world's first ever photograph, showing a simple window, was taken in 1825 by the French inventor Joseph Niépce. After 1839, technology developed to allow for more creative and clearer pictures of people and places. By the 1900s, companies such as Francis Frith & Co. and Kodak were producing pictures from all over the world.

In 1975, the US engineer Steven Sasson invented and built the first electronic camera while working for Kodak. By the late 1990s, digital cameras were in common use. But it was the mobile phone, especially the smartphone, that brought digital photography to the masses. By 2012, Samsung estimated that 2.5 out of 7 billion of the world's population had a digital camera.

Camera phones have transformed the way we live. People take photographs of everything from restaurant meals to football matches and music concerts. The rise of the 'selfie' generation has been motivated by, among other things, a desire to share experiences, record 'I was there' and seek attention. The digital camera has empowered new citizen journalists who record world events, such as 9/11 or the fall of dictators, which are then immediately shared on social media.

Photography has gone from being a pastime for the very rich to an everyday part of our lives.

Did you know?

■ Smartphones are used to take three out of four photos in the world.

■ In 2017, it is estimated that 1.2 trillion digital photos were taken (1,200,000,000,000).

■ The world record for the most number of people taking selfies at the same time is 4,991 – it was organised by the Younique Foundation (USA) in 2016.

■ The record for the most consecutive photographs taken of a person was achieved by Munish Bansal, who took photos of his daughter Suman every day until her eighteenth birthday. He has 6,575 photos in his collection.

■ In 2015, it was reported that a staggering 24 billion selfies were uploaded to Google Photos.

■ In 2015, there were more selfie deaths than deaths due to shark attacks.

Ready

■ **Key resources**: digital camera, tablet/smartphone.

■ **Health and safety**: remember confidentiality and privacy when using photographs in educational settings. Parent or guardian permission is needed to take and display pictures of young children, so ensure that parents provide written permission to take and show pictures of their children. Be careful not to display any pictures of children without the consent of their parents and do not upload photographs that can identify individuals to the Internet if public access is possible. For those children who are not allowed to be photographed or who may have difficult family backgrounds, ensure that you have suitable alternative activities available.

■ **Key vocabulary**: digital, camera, technology, upload, edit, transfer, file, disk, print.

Steady

Young children can be taught the essentials of photography quickly and simply. They often prefer to use a camera designed for adults rather than one specifically for children. Disposable cameras are a good option for using with very young children, for sending home and for use in the outdoors, and digital cameras that plug straight into a computer via a USB make downloading very simple.

Before teaching, reflect on the following goals/learning intentions:

■ To develop independence and decision making as children choose to capture special moments.

■ To promote self-esteem and encourage children to be at the centre of their learning through choosing who and what they photograph.

■ To develop language skills by holding conversations about photos.

■ To know how to use a digital camera.

Go

Activity 1: Personalised books

Ask the children to use photographs to create a book that is unique to your setting. For example, they could develop language skills by taking photographs of objects and places in your school that represent each letter of the alphabet and then arrange these into an alphabet book (either an e-book using an app such as Book Creator or a hard copy). Extend this by including photos of children whose names begin with each letter or set a challenge as a home–school activity – for example, send home a disposable camera with the challenge to find and photograph three foods which start with the letter 'p'. Focusing on one letter and resourcing the provision to allow plenty of opportunities to find objects to photograph starting with that letter could simplify this activity, or consider numbers (e.g. three flowers, two cats, three bags), colours, shapes or sizes to extend it.

Activity 2: Signs and symbols

Take a small group of children on a walk around the school's local area. Allow them to find and choose signs, symbols and logos that interest them, and then encourage the children to work with a partner and photograph them. These could be letters, numbers or images. Print these out and then talk about them as a group. What are the signs and symbols for? What colours, design features and so on can they see? What do they like or dislike about them? Can they group them and look for similarities and differences? Use the photos to create a display of the locality. You could extend this to labelling a large-scale map of the area with some of the images, or the photos could provide a starting point for retelling the journey.

Activity 3: That's me in the picture

In James Mayhew's series of books (e.g. *Katie in London*, 2003; *Katie and the British Artists*, 2008), Katie is a little girl who finds herself exploring famous paintings as they come to life. Children can use these celebrated works of art as a starting point for discussion. They can then use digital cameras to take photographs of themselves which can be added to the artwork – either on a computer and then printed or using cut-out images that are stuck onto copies of the painting. This can be the starting point for some fabulous story-telling, role play and dramatic activities, such as freeze-frames, and could be extended to some green-screen activities using the painting as the backdrop for an adventure.

Activity 4: Mix and match

Take full height pictures of the children, adults in the setting and willing parents so that you have heads, torsos and legs in shot. Print these off as A5 images – they all need to be the same size and in the same proportion. Laminate them, cut them into three equal sections (each photo needs to be cut in the same place) and bind them together into a flip book. Now the children can get creative, mixing and matching heads, bodies and legs. You could extend this to add images of soft toys and cartoon characters into the mix. This can be the starting point for some creative writing. Robinson and Sharatt's *Mixed Up Fairy Tales* (2005) gives further inspiration to this idea and connects to familiar tales.

Other ideas

- **Create a 'then and now' display of children and teachers when they were babies**: can they guess who is who? Match the baby photos to recent photos. What is similar or different? What has changed and what has stayed the same? Encourage the children and adults to write about their favourite baby food, toys or other memories.

- **Explore age-appropriate apps and augmented reality**: HP Reveal (formerly Aurasma) is an augmented reality app which allows 2D images to be brought to life by linking them to video/3D images. For example, the children could be recorded talking about their artwork so that when you scan the piece of art you hear their description. Morfo allows a photograph to be turned into a talking 3D character. Quick response (QR) codes can be used to provide instructions or information about an aspect of provision.

- **Get creative**: image transfer fluid allows photographs to be transferred onto wood, glass, plastic, fabric and so on. This allows for photos to be used for creative displays, self-registering, gifts for special events and signs for indoor and outdoor provision.

Find out more

■ There are thirteen titles in James Mayhew's Katie series including *Katie and the Dinosaurs* (1991), *Katie and the Impressionists* (1997) and *Katie and the Starry Night* (2012).

■ Image transfer fluid is readily available online.

■ Find out more about the augmented reality app HP Reveal at: www. hpreveal.com.

E is for Eggs, Egg Timers and Egg Boxes

In a nutshell

Humans have been eating eggs for thousands of years, with archaeological evidence for egg consumption dating back to the Neolithic period. By 3200 BC, jungle fowl had been domesticated in India. The Romans enjoyed the eggs of many birds, including peacocks, and brought egg-laying hens to England, Gaul and Germany. Egg timers have been used since the 1300s to check whether food was cooked. The first domesticated fowl reached North America with the second voyage of Columbus in 1493.

In the nineteenth century, egg collecting was very popular. Many collections of blown eggs were eventually displayed in museums. However, since 1954 changes in the law have made it illegal to take the eggs of any wild bird.

Until the 1920s, most people carried eggs in baskets. The egg carton or box was invented in 1911 by a newspaper editor to resolve a dispute between a farmer in British Columbia and a hotel manager who complained about broken eggs.

Since ancient times, eggs have been symbolic of new life and associated with magical beliefs. The egg is used by Christians at Easter to represent new life. In 2018, the National Trust caused controversy when it dropped the word 'Easter' from its annual egg hunt for children. The organisation reversed the decision following public outrage.

Eggs are not only laid by birds but by many species of animals including amphibians, reptiles and fish. They come in different sizes, colours and shell types. This means there is plenty to explore and engage learners, whether from fact or fantasy.

Did you know?

- The largest hen egg on record was laid by a Black Minorca in Lancashire in 1896, measuring 31 cm in diameter, but the heaviest (454 g) is reported to have been laid by a hen in the United States in 1956.

- The largest egg and spoon race on record had 1,445 participants and involved participants from Morecambe Community High School in Lancashire in 2012.

- The smallest egg laid by any bird is that of the vervain hummingbird of Jamaica – typically only 10 mm in length.

- The tallest chocolate Easter egg measured 10.39 metres in height and was made in Italy in 2011.

- The most Cadbury Creme Eggs eaten in one minute is six, achieved by Canadian Pete Czerwinski in 2014.

- The most people dipping egg soldiers simultaneously is 178 and was achieved by soldiers of the Allied Rapid Response Corps in Gloucestershire in 2014.

- Charles Bendire, an American ornithologist and army major, once braved enemy fire to capture a rare hawk's egg from a tree. He cushioned it in his mouth while he galloped to safety. Back at camp, he discovered the egg was stuck in his mouth because his jaw had tensed and swelled. He ordered his men to remove the egg intact, although they broke one of his teeth in the process.

Ready

- **Key resources**: hard-boiled eggs, food dyes, vinegar (Activity 1); plastic eggs, egg boxes (Activity 2); egg boxes, cubes, etc. (Activity 3); collection of recipes (Activity 4); egg timers (Activity 5).

- **Health and safety**: when working with eggs, egg boxes or egg shells ensure that none of the children in your class have an egg allergy.

- **Key vocabulary**: box, carton, basket, egg, chicken, Easter, birds, small/large, boil, runny, dry, hunt, collect, ornithologist.

Steady

Before teaching, reflect on the following goals/learning intentions:

- To develop everyday language when talking about measures.

- To use and explore a variety of materials, tools and techniques, experimenting with colour, design, texture, form and function.

- To use phonic knowledge to decode regular words and read them aloud accurately.

Go

Activity 1: Egg decorator

Hard-boiled eggs can be dyed in a liquid made from half a cup of water, one teaspoon of white vinegar and about twenty drops of food colouring. Submerge the egg and leave for at least five minutes. Experiment with leaving it for longer or shorter times (it makes the colour lighter or darker), using different colours and then paint with acrylic paint, adding glitter, feathers and other decorations. Find inspiration for decoration online – for example, Ukrainian eggs.

Activity 2: Word family fun

Collect some two-part plastic eggs and use these to practise word families with the children. For example, when looking at consonant, vowel, consonant (CVC) words such as 'cat', 'mat' and 'hat', label the two halves of the egg – one half of the egg has the end of the word (stem), while the other has the initial sound. Keep these in egg boxes labelled according to the word family to which the eggs belong. How many words can the children make in a minute? How quickly can they read the words? Can they put the words into a sentence?

Activity 3: Egg box number recognition

Label the holes of an egg box with appropriate numbers for the age of the learners. For example, older children could be given a fifteen-egg box with each hole labelled with numbers in the two times table, while younger learners could be given a four-egg box labelled with the digits 1–4. Mark cubes/buttons/counters/wrapped sweets with matching digits and see if the children can place the cubes into the correct holes (using tweezers to develop their fine motor skills). You could also use plastic eggs: write a number on one half and the equivalent number of dots on the other, which the children should then match. Extend this by, for example, placing set numbers of counters in each egg and then getting the children to match these to the correct holes in the egg box.

Activity 4: Eggsellent recipes

It would be a shame to do a great deal of work on egg boxes without eating some eggs! There are numerous recipes to try, from cakes and meringues to omelettes. Try a simple recipe for 'one eye jack' found in the Boy Scouts of America handbook (1990): use an upside-down cup to cut a hole out of the centre of a slice of bread. Lay the bread in a hot, oiled pan and crack an egg into the hole. Fry it for a few minutes until the egg sets, then flip the bread and egg with a spatula and cook the other side. You'll have an egg and toast all in one. This would be even more exciting if the holes were shaped using cookie cutters and if the food was cooked outdoors in a forest school setting!

Activity 5: How long is a minute?

Talk to the children about time and think about whether we can see time, how we know what time it is and why time is so important. Discuss how we can see time passing on a clock. What would people do if there were no clocks? Collect some egg timers and encourage the children to estimate one minute. Set up some challenges around your provision – for example, how many cards can they match/cubes can they collect/star jumps can they do in a minute? Encourage the children to make a prediction and then have a go. Do their predictions get better with practice?

Other ideas

- ■ **Create an egg box garden**: egg cartons are perfect as seed starters. Just fill each cup with potting compost and plant some seeds – quick growing ones like cress or sunflowers are ideal. If you are going to plant these outdoors, just tear the bottom of the carton and plant them directly in the ground.

■ **Light an egg box fire in the forest school**: with adult supervision, fill each section of the egg box with melted wax and other materials such as kindling, straw or shredded paper. When you want to start a fire, rip off one of the egg cups, light the box part and you have an easy way to get the fire going.

■ **Arrange a traditional egg and spoon race**: not just for sports day! Combine egg timers and egg boxes and hold an egg and spoon race. Get the children to design and make special spoons from egg boxes and estimate how far they can get in a minute. Compare the egg carton spoon with a normal spoon, and talk about which is better and why.

■ **Eggimals**: use hard-boiled eggs and different foods to get creative and make animals such as pegguins, eggapotamuses and eggodiles for a picnic. For example, an eggosaurus could be made by attaching an olive or grape using a toothpick to one end of the egg, digging small eye holes and inserting raisins or seeds, surrounding the head with broccoli florets, making a slit down the back and filling it with a row of tortillas, adding celery legs and a long carrot stick tail.

Find out more

■ The Incredible Egg website has an eggcyclopedia of facts and figures all about eggs: www.incredibleegg.org.

F is for Feathers

In a nutshell

Feathers are unique to birds (and most dinosaur species). They are highly specialised and serve a number of functions – from protecting the bird from sun, rain and cold, to providing camouflage, displaying social dominance and attracting a mate. Different types of feathers serve a different purpose – for example, sensory feathers provide information about wind and air pressure, contour feathers are critical for flight and down feathers offer warmth.

Just like our fingernails, feathers are made of a lightweight material called keratin. The feathers are attached to muscles which allow the bird to move them around. Each feather has a central hollow shaft with a flat area either side – called the vane. The bare part at the base of the shaft is called the quill. The vane has many small side branches. These are all linked together by even smaller branches with hooks, called barbules.

A bird keeps its feathers tidy by 'zipping up' the barbules on each one with its bill. When you examine a feather closely you can 'zip' and 'unzip' it for yourself.

Did you know?

■ In 2000, a 220-million-year-old fossilised feathered animal, named *Longisquama insignis,* was discovered. Scientists believe that the creature used its feathers to glide between trees 75 million years before the first birds evolved.

■ The bird with the largest vocabulary is a budgerigar called Oskar from Germany. He can say 148 words.

■ The oldest duck on record was a female mallard called Desi from the UK who lived to be twenty years, three months and sixteen days before she died in 2002.

■ The most canned drinks opened in one minute by a bird is thirty-five, achieved by a macaw called Zac from the United States in 2012.

■ The largest dreamcatcher on record is 7.42 metres in diameter, and was made by a Russian, Mamaeva Bibigul, in 2016. The dreamcatcher was made of willow branches and jute rope and decorated with beads and feathers.

Ready

■ **Key resources**: feathers (we suggest sourcing cruelty-free feathers (available online) which are collected during natural moulting or finding feathers of your own while out walking; alternatively, opt for artificial versions (again, widely available online)); pasta, sequins and other materials (Activity 1); copies of Chris Maynard's artwork (Activity 2); old yoghurt pots or large pine cones, bird food, raisins, peanuts, grated cheese, suet/lard (Activity 3); large feathers, natural materials, beads, ribbon (Activity 4).

■ **Health and safety**: take appropriate steps regarding personal hygiene – always wash hands after touching feathers and never pick feathers from a dead bird. Some children may be allergic to feathers so check this in advance.

■ **Key vocabulary**: feather, quill, vane, shaft, keratin, budgerigar, macaw.

Steady

Before teaching, reflect on the following goals/learning intentions:

■ To develop control and coordination in large and small movements.

■ To experiment with colour, design, texture, form and function.

■ To represent ideas through design and technology, art, music and using technology for a purpose.

Go

Activity 1: Peacock sculptures

Explore the beautiful peacock through images – and if possible through a real-life encounter. Use newspaper to shape peacock models – rolling, scrunching, pinching and taping together. Wrap the paper model carefully in layers of ModRoc. Once dry these can be decorated and painted for a fabulous display. Alternatively, press modelling clay onto cardboard to create 3D peacocks – use pasta, sequins and other materials to represent its beautiful feathers.

Activity 2: Feather mosaic

Feathers are beautiful and varied. Use Chris Maynard's artwork (http://www. featherfolio.com/shadow-boxes) as a stimulus and create your own displays, using ICT to record the artwork for display. Talk about shape, colour, size, pattern, texture and orientation of the feathers. Ask the children to zoom in on a favourite feather and explore it under a microscope or magnifying glass, and then draw what they see.

Activity 3: Banquets for birds

Create exciting and nutritious food for your local birds. Use good quality bird seed and mix with raisins, peanuts, grated cheese, suet or lard. Place the mix into recycled yoghurt pots, or alternatively spread the mix onto large pine cones. Place the cakes outside and tally up the birds that come to feast. Get the children to use a bird-spotting guide to start to identify them and note what times of day they visit. Extend by making different varieties of cake (e.g. a nut and seed variety or a fruit variety) and see what the birds prefer. Use natural food colourings to see if the birds in your school garden have a preferred colour of cake.

Activity 4: Talking pieces

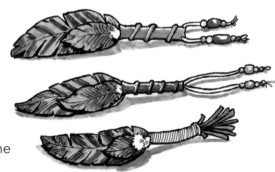

In many First Nation cultures, sharing stories around a fire has always been an important part of life. To ensure that all voices were heard, they sat in circles and used a 'talking piece' to pass from individual to individual. This ensured that everyone had a turn to speak. The talking pieces were usually made from natural and beautiful materials, so get the children to use beads and ribbon to decorate large and ornate feathers to create talking pieces of your own, and pass these around during circle time and group tasks.

Other ideas

■ **You ate what?** For older children, examining owl pellets can be a fascinating piece of detective work. Pellets are small and contain the undigested parts of the bird's food which are ejected through the mouth. Pellets are not droppings so they do not smell and are not unpleasant to work with. They consist of things like the bones of birds, mammals and fish; teeth, claws and beaks; insect head parts and wing cases; seed husks; and other indigestible materials. These are usually enclosed by softer material like fur, feathers and vegetable fibre. You can dissect pellets with tweezers and cocktail sticks when they are dry or you can soak them in a little water first.

■ **Build a bowerbird nest**: bowerbirds decorate their nests in beautiful and complex ways to attract a mate. Examine these via the Internet or non-fiction books. Then go into the outdoors and build nests from twigs, leaves and other natural materials  and then decorate them with natural and recycled materials (remember to take these home at the end of the day). Challenge children to make a nest for a very small bird (e.g. wren or hummingbird) or a very large one (e.g. eagle or swan).

■ **Build a bird house**: young children can be taught to use simple woodworking tools and will enjoy measuring, hammering nails and sawing pieces of wood to create a house for birds. This could be an ideal opportunity for some community engagement with DIY-keen parents or grandparents coming in to help or an afterschool club with older children. If a bird house seems ambitious, a bird table may be more manageable, especially if you create a tray-sized one to hang from a branch.

Find out more

- Buy owl pellets from the Barn Owl Trust: http://www.barnowltrust.org.uk/ product/pellet-dissection-pack.

- Take part in the RSPB's Birdwatch scheme: https://ww2.rspb.org.uk/ kids-and-schools/kids-at-school/schools-birdwatch.

G is for Glasses (and Goblets)

In a nutshell

Glassmaking is the process of shaping molten glass by blowing air into the glass through a tube. It has a very long history. Around 4,000 years ago, glass containers were made by covering a sand core with a layer of molten glass. The Romans brought glassmaking to Britain and they also recycled broken glass. The British Museum has examples of Roman goblets featuring tiny silver and gold particles (less than one-thousandth of the size of a grain of table salt), showing remarkable nanotechnological skills.

Glassworking spread with the growth of the Roman Empire. Many churches in the Middle Ages had stained-glass windows made of pieces of coloured glass held together in a latticed web of lead. Some of the best and oldest surviving examples can be seen in the cathedrals at Augsburg (Germany), Chartres (France) and York Minster.

George Ravenscroft, a seventeenth-century glassworks owner, added lead to crystal glass which gave a sparkling, bright appearance which 'rings' when struck.

Glass is now widely used for practical, decorative and technological purposes such as window panes, tableware and optoelectronics.

Glass is 100% recyclable, without loss of quality or purity. Many people associate glass with quality. Concerns over plastic pollution have seen increased sales of glass products and services, including a return of the old-fashioned milkman and the fresh pint delivered on the doorstep.

Did you know?

- In 1851, a special building called the Crystal Palace was erected to celebrate British achievements, using 300,000 sheets of the largest glass ever made (1.3 m x 25.3 cm).

- Crystal Palace Football Club is named after the glasshouse site and was formed by workers who put up the glass and iron building.

- On average, every family in the UK uses around 330 glass bottles and jars each year.

- A 'gob' is a molten lump of glass to which a glass blower attached a tube to blow the glass into shape. The blower had to blow hard which made his cheeks very large. Today someone with a big mouth is told they have a big gob – hence the expression, 'Shut yer gob'.

- The largest plastic cup pyramid used 56,980 cups and was created by Kushagra Tayal in India on 17 September 2016. The pyramid had fifty-five layers and was 6.6 metres tall.

- The game of marbles using glass balls has been popular for centuries.

Ready

- **Key resources**: Plastic glasses are readily available in a wide range of shapes, colours and sizes in supermarkets, bargain stores and online. Large glass, lemonade, raisins/currants (Activity 1); range of fruits, vegetables and yoghurts (Activity 2); tall glasses, small clear bottles, liquids (bubble bath, syrup, oil, glue, etc.) (Activity 3); variety of glasses and goblets, modelling clay (Activity 4).

- **Health and safety**: when decorating cups, take care around the rim so there is no danger of the children swallowing any materials (e.g. sequins, glitter, beads).

- **Key vocabulary**: glass, goblet, plastic, recycle, transparent, blow, tall, liquid, stained glass.

Steady

Before you start, reflect on the following goals/learning intentions:

- To explore a variety of materials, tools and techniques.

- To represent ideas, thoughts and feelings through design and technology and art.

- To look closely and respond in a variety of ways to what is seen, smelled, touched and felt.

- To know the importance of good health and a healthy diet.

Go

Activity 1: Fizzy fun

Pour some lemonade into a large, clear glass (don't use a diet lemonade – the reaction works better with the original version). Look closely at the bubbles. Where do they start? Where do they go? Can the children describe them? Pour some tap water into another glass. Does it look the same? Now take a few raisins and currants of different sizes. Get the children to examine them carefully and describe how they feel, smell and taste. What do they think will happen when the dried fruits are added to the liquids, and will the same thing happen in both glasses? The bubbles of gas in the lemonade cause the raisins to bob up and down in the glass, providing lots of discussion opportunities. Older children may like to time how quickly big and small raisins bob to the surface, and discuss why.

Activity 2: Smoothie superstore

Bring in different fruits, vegetables and yoghurts. Get the children to use all their senses to explore them – sorting and grouping them by, for example, colour, whether they have seeds, whether they are soft or crunchy. Carry out taste tests, vote on which are most popular and tally up the results. Decide which ones could be combined to make super smoothies. Ask the children to think about how to combine these into smoothies, what ingredients would go together well and how they could get green or red smoothies. Use the opportunity to talk about healthy eating and explore vocabulary related to tastes, colours and textures. Take photos of the finished smoothies. Encourage the children to talk or write about the recipe. Look at packaging (perhaps visit a local shop to look at branding) and describe the smoothies using exciting vocabulary (e.g. 'Tasty Tastebud Tingler'). Smoothies could then be made for an event (e.g. school fair or parent assembly) and sold, developing a range of literacy, numeracy and creative thinking skills. You could also create adverts for the smoothies using digital technology.

Activity 3: Races in a glass

Fill tall, thin glasses with different liquids (e.g. water, bubble bath, syrup, oil, glue). Ask the children to describe the liquid (e.g. thick, runny, gooey) and compare similarities and differences. Pour each liquid into a small clear bottle (such as a travel-sized toiletries bottle), leaving a small gap at the top. Turn each bottle upside down to show how a bubble forms. Observe bubbles moving through liquids of different viscosity. Tilt the bottle at different angles to see whether that makes a difference. Can the children predict which bubble will win the race if all the bottles are turned upside down at the same time? Can they transfer their thinking if a new liquid is introduced?

Activity 4: Clay sculpture

Clay is a rich natural play experience for young children. It is soft and responsive and the children can poke it, squeeze it, hit it, pinch it and pound it. Manipulating a piece of clay develops children's large and small motor skills and also fosters eye–hand coordination. Provide a collection of glasses and goblets for the children to explore and then encourage them to create their own from clay. These can be dried and decorated.

Other ideas

- **Bubbly drinks**: mix six teaspoons of citric acid crystals (available from pharmacies) with three teaspoons of baking soda. Mix and grind until this forms a powder, then add two tablespoons of icing sugar (the icing sugar takes away the sour taste, so add up to four tablespoons accordingly). This creates your fizzy powder. When added to still drinks, such as orange juice, the chemical reaction between the dissolving citric acid and baking soda releases bubbles of carbon dioxide. Hey presto, a magic fizzy potion! You can also eat the powder directly, which causes a fizzy feeling on your tongue.

- **Kings and queens**: use imaginative play to plan a party for a king and queen or for a visit from a character from a favourite story. Prepare the role play area or a picnic blanket outside ready for the visitors. Lay the table or places accordingly – how many plates, glasses, knives and forks will you need? Take the visitors' orders when they arrive.

Find out more

- Watch videos on glassmaking (e.g. https://www.youtube.com/watch?v=XxgIEeIBCFo) including the magic of making glass marbles (e.g. https://www.youtube.com/watch?v=1cXy7gxUtbU).

- Encourage the children to talk to older relatives about the game of marbles and discuss marble terminology such as 'bombies', 'keepsies', 'quitsies' and 'shooters'.

H is for Hoops

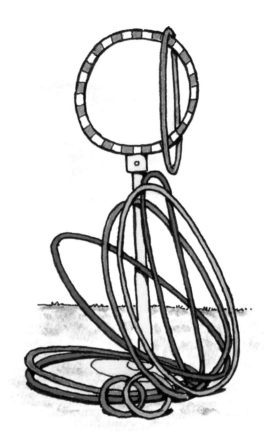

In a nutshell

Hoops have universal appeal through time and place. As toys, the ancient Egyptians curved reeds and rattan to form hoops which they threw into the air, swung around their waists or pushed along the ground with a stick.

Cheap plastic toy hoops started to appear in the 1950s and became instantly popular. However, in Russia they were banned as an example of 'the emptiness of American culture' (Mansour, 2005: 229) and in Japan they were considered indecent.

Hoops have been used for other purposes. The ancient Greeks used their grapevine hoops as exercise equipment, while Eskimo children practised harpoon throwing through hoops.

Hoops also have spiritual significance. For Lakota Native Americans the hoop symbolises the Circle of Life. Their Hoop Dance can feature up to thirty hoops as the storyteller transforms himself into animals and other elements in the story.

Today, hoops are used around the world by people of all ages – for example, there are websites and videos featuring those in their nineties enjoying this ancient pastime.

Did you know?

■ The actual name 'hoop' originated when British sailors visited the Hawaiian Islands. The sailors were impressed by the traditional hula dance, recognised the similar hip movements and hence the name 'hula hoop' was born.

■ Ashrita Furman managed to hula hoop underwater for 2 minutes and 38 seconds in August 2007.

■ Aaron Hibbs of the United States holds the record for the longest continuous hula hooping. He managed 74 hours and 54 minutes in 2009.

■ The highest hula hooping on record was carried out on the top of Mount Kilimanjaro in 2010.

■ In 2015, Marawa Ibrahim twirled a total of 200 hula hoops at one time in Australia to become the record holder for the most hula hoops to be twirled at once.

Ready

■ **Key resources**: large and small hoops (Activity 1); hoops, coloured beanbags (Activity 2); blank dice, hoops (Activity 3); plastic hoops, strips of fabric (Activity 4).

■ **Health and safety**: ensure the children have enough space and access to the right size hoops. The child must be able to stand up and hold the hula hoop in front of him or her.

■ **Key vocabulary**: hoop, sideways, left/right, sequence, low/high, underarm/overarm, circle, workout.

Steady

Before teaching, reflect on the following goals/learning intentions:

■ To handle correctly a range of small and large equipment.

■ To move confidently in a range of ways.

■ To work well as part of a group or class, taking turns and sharing fairly.

■ To recognise numbers up to five.

Go

Activity 1: Hula hoop circus

Crawling, stretching and jumping through hoops offers excellent opportunities to develop gross motor skills and some creative thinking. Hold the hoop up vertically while it is still resting on the ground and get the children to climb through. Lift the hoop up a bit and see if they can change the way they move to get through. Ask the children to put their right leg through first or right arm and left leg. Give variations on which body part(s) to place into the hoop first. Hold the hoop horizontally and try the same tasks. Have the children move through a sequence of hoops – one could be vertical, the next horizontal, then one raised higher or lower and so on. Space the hoops apart at different distances. Can they jump from one to another or only place one foot on the ground between hoops? Can they spin the hoops on their legs and arms or around their waist? Can they roll it along the floor? Can they prepare a sequence of three movements and perform these for their partner?

Activity 2: Hoopla

Place three different coloured hoops in a triangle shape. Gather a collection of beanbags of the same colours. Can the children throw the correct coloured beanbags into the hoops? How many beanbags land in each hoop? Can they throw with both hands? Underarm? Overarm? What happens if they take a step back? Extend by placing a cone with a small ball on the top in the middle of each hoop – can they knock the ball off?

Activity 3: Number wheels

Label a blank dice with numbers appropriate for your children. Place the same number of hoops on the ground, each labelled with a numeral. Roll the dice and ask the children to stand in the matching hoop. Can the correct number of children stand in the hoop (e.g. three children in the 'three' hoop if the dice rolls three)? Can they then find the matching numeral from a collection of wooden/foam/plastic numerals? Which is the largest number? The smallest? What comes next?

Activity 4: Hoop weaving

Use a plastic hoop as the frame. Cut up some old T-shirts into loops of fabric around 2 cm wide. You will need six or seven T-shirts in total. Stretch the first strip across the hoop. Then take a second piece and stretch it across perpendicular to the first, creating a cross shape. Continue until you have stretched ten or eleven strips around the hoop, like spokes. Take your first fabric loop 'weft' and secure it around the centre of one of the spokes. Weave over and under each warp spoke in a circle, making sure it fits quite snugly. To finish, simply cut the end of the loop and tie around the nearest spoke. For a tutorial see: https://www.youtube.com/watch?v=AZsSg7zUo9c.

Other ideas

- **Pass the hoop**: ask the children to stand in a circle holding hands. Place a hoop between two children and encourage them to pass the hoop around the circle without letting go of each other's hands. This encourages cooperation and problem solving.

- **Photo frames and story boards**: tie colourful ribbons tightly across a hoop to create a series of mini 'washing lines'. Use colourful pegs to attach photos, drawings or parts of a story so the hoop becomes a display board.

- **Odds and evens basketball**: attach two hoops to the board or wall as if they are basketball hoops, one to be labelled 'odds' and one 'evens'. Use wooden numerals, number cards, etc. and encourage the children to shoot these into the correct hoop.

Find out more

- Visit the Hooping website for ideas and examples of world-class performances to inspire the children: http://www.hooping.org/about.

- Inspire children with videos of LED or fibre optic hoop displays (e.g. https://www.youtube.com/watch?v=S2jvrRr0M8M). How many colours can they identify?

I is for Ice Cubes

In a nutshell

Ice is water in its frozen state. As water cools, the amount of potential energy is reduced and the molecules start to move more slowly. When the water temperature reaches around 0° Celsius (32° Fahrenheit) the molecules stick together and form a solid – ice.

Around 10% of the Earth's land area is covered in ice and 75% of fresh water is stored in glaciers – huge blocks of ice. Almost all of these are to be found in Greenland and Antarctica. These glaciers formed over millions of years during long periods (ice ages) when the planet's temperatures fell.

Throughout history, ice has been used for building homes, as a source of leisure and to keep food from spoiling. The earliest experiments with ice cream were carried out by the Persians around 500 BC, who poured concentrated grape juice over snow. By the 1800s, the wealthy had ice cut from lakes in winter and stored in the ground or brick ice houses which were insulated with straw.

In the nineteenth century, US railways had special carriages in which meat was suspended over ice and salt to keep it fresh. Drinks could also be kept cool. In 1914, an ice cube box was included for the first time in a refrigerating machine. But it was not until the 1920s and 1930s that it became common for electric refrigerators to come with a freezer section that included an ice cube compartment with trays. Modern designers are continually trying to think of new ideas for ice cube trays, such as those shaped as animals and quick-release tabs for individual cubes.

Did you know?

■ The world's first ice hotel was built in 1990, in the village of Jukkasjärvi in Sweden. There are now ice hotels to be found across Scandinavia, Canada and Japan. They are rebuilt every year.

■ The world's largest glacier in Antarctica is more than 96 km wide and 435 km long. It measures 2,500 metres deep at its centre (more than eight times the height of the tallest building in the UK, the Shard).

■ DNA drawn from Ötzi the Iceman, a 5,000-year-old mummy discovered in an Alpine glacier, reveals that he has nineteen living genetic relatives in Austria.

■ Some snowflakes are made of a single ice crystal while others are made of as many as 200 ice crystals fused together.

■ The Inupiaq people of Alaska have more than 100 names for different kinds of sea ice.

Ready

■ **Key resources**: ice cube trays, juice, flowers/leaves/berries, photos of ice hotels and igloos (Activity 1); ice cube trays, jelly, butter, chocolate, greaseproof paper, pens, camera (Activity 2); natural treasures, plastic containers, cookie cutters, string (Activity 3); ice cube trays, small world characters, hairdryer/torch/towels (Activity 4).

■ **Health and safety**: ensure that you remain aware of children's fingers when handling ice – use gloves if appropriate and do not handle for long periods.

■ **Key vocabulary**: ice, ice cubes, tray, melt, freeze, solid, temperature, glacier.

Steady

Before teaching, reflect on the following goals/learning intentions:

■ To safely explore a variety of materials, tools and techniques.

■ To develop vocabulary to describe ice (e.g. its appearance, feel, size and shape).

■ To investigate materials using all the senses and to look closely at change.

Go

Activity 1: Flower, leaf and berry building blocks

Get the children to pour juice of different colours or place small berries or chopped herbs into ice cube trays and freeze overnight. Flowers can also be placed in each compartment. Look at images of ice houses, igloos and ice hotels and discuss with the children how they are made, and who might live in them. Place the cubes in the small world play area to construct walls, houses and so on (or in the mathematics area to create patterns or for grouping and classifying) and invite the children to take photos of the buildings. Talk about the size and shape as they build.

Activity 2: Melting is messy

Ice cube trays can be used to make cubes of ice, jelly, hard butter and chocolate. Explore these using the senses – for example, how do they feel? Smell? Taste? Ask the children to place one of each cube on a piece of greaseproof paper and draw around it. Repeat so they have three or four sets of cubes. Leave the sheets of paper in different places around the setting (e.g. in the sun, in the shade, by the radiator) and return in five minutes. What has happened? Talk about melting and consider which things have melted the most. Get the children to touch the cubes to see if they feel different. Draw around them now, return in five minutes and repeat. Take some photos and sequence them to show the process of melting. Extend by asking what might happen when we put the cubes in the fridge, and explore this to see what happens. Do the cubes reform or harden in their new shapes?

Activity 3: Ice pictures

Collect some exciting objects and treasures from the outdoors – leaves, flowers, seeds, etc. Get the children to arrange the objects inside cookie cutters which have been placed inside food containers, and then gently add water. They should place a loop of string so that one end is within the cutter, and then freeze them overnight. These decorations can be loosened from the container with warm water and then hung around the outdoor provision as beautiful decorations. You can extend this to use food colouring or objects such as shells, feathers or beads. The children can revisit the decorations during the day to see what happens to them.

Activity 4: Set me free

Freeze small world characters in ice cube trays and other small containers overnight. Explain to the children that they have become trapped and need our help to free them. Talk about how they could be released – that is, what is needed to melt the ice? Give the children (with appropriate supervision) the choice of, for example, a hairdryer, a bowl of warm water, torches or towels and allow them to explore what works well. Extend the activity by making and testing predictions, and timing how long it takes to set the characters free.

Other ideas

- **Parts of a penguin**: gather some stuffed toy penguins or model penguins and watch a video of penguins in the wild (there are lots to choose from on sites like YouTube). Take time to explore these and label body parts – bill, eyes, flipper, claws, etc. Talk about what each body part is for and why the penguin needs them. Compare penguins to flamingos and magpies, and discuss similarities and differences.

- **Pick up a penguin**: hide a range of plastic eggs around the setting in advance. Learn about penguin parenting by reading *The Emperor's Egg* by Martin Jenkins (1999). Talk about how male penguins huddle together and balance the eggs on their feet to protect them from the cold. Encourage the children to find the eggs you have hidden around the class, count and sort them and then huddle together, keeping the eggs balanced on their toes. Can they walk like a penguin? To feel even more like a penguin, ask them to make and wear a penguin mask, wear black and white clothes and, to protect the egg, tie a small pillow to their waist with a belt and use this like the penguin's tummy.

- **Penguin snow globe**: Pinterest (www.pinterest.co.uk) has lots of creative ideas for making snow globes, including ones with penguins made from pipe cleaners, cardboard tubes, Christmas cards or modelling clay.

Find out more

- Research ice sculptures and competitions – for example, the World Ice Art Championships in Alaska and the Harbin Ice Festival in China.

- Find out more about frozen works of art that are carved from solid blocks of ice and snow in places such as Siberia, Canada and Japan.

J is for Jam Jars

In a nutshell

Fruit preserves are essentially a mix of fruit and sugar that has been boiled so that it will set. There are different kinds of preserves. Jam, marmalade, curd, compote and jelly differ in their consistency, texture, colour, flavour and clarity. *The Telegraph* reported in 2012 that sales of jam and marmalade have declined, losing out to trendier spreads like peanut butter and chocolate.

The Romans provided the first cookbooks which featured recipes for jams. The ingredients were soft fruit heated with sugar or honey, which were then left to cool and stored. In 1785, a French chef called Nicolas Appert won a competition to preserve food for the French army by using sealed containers. In 1858, John Mason invented a jar which had a rubber ring on the underside of the lid to create an airtight seal to preserve the food. Today some of these antique jars sell for several hundred pounds.

Jam and marmalade are not the same thing. In England, marmalade usually refers to preserves made using citrus fruits, while jam refers to all other fruits. Since 2005, the World's Original Marmalade Awards have been held in Cumbria. In 2018, the winner, from Cornwall, produced a jar of grapefruit and gin marmalade.

Throughout history, honey has been highly regarded as a medicine, thought to help with everything from sore throats and digestive disorders to skin problems and hay fever. Honey has antiseptic properties and was historically used as a dressing for wounds and a first aid treatment for burns and cuts. It is the only food that keeps indefinitely.

Did you know?

- The first marmalades weren't actually made from oranges. The word marmalade comes from *marmelo*, the Portuguese word for quince.

- Joan of Arc ate quince jam before going into battle as it filled her with courage.

- Jam was introduced to Scotland by Queen Mary Stewart in 1560, after her French husband died. She ate the jam when she felt sick!

- A popular myth is that marmalade came to Britain in 1700, when a storm-damaged Spanish ship, carrying Seville oranges, sought refuge in Dundee harbour. James Keiller, a local merchant, bought the cargo cheaply and his wife turned it into a preserve.

- To mark its 125th birthday in 2006, jam makers F. Duerr & Sons created the world's most expensive jar of marmalade containing whisky, vintage champagne and edible gold leaf. It cost £5,000 – the equivalent of £76 per slice of toast!

- In 2008, Paddington Bear 'wrote' *My Book of Marmalade*.

- 'Elvish' honey from caves in Turkey costs 5,000 euros per kilogram.

Ready

- **Key resources**: jam jars and appropriate ingredients (Activity 1); bee video (Activity 2); 'Flight of the Bumblebee' music, ribbons (Activity 3); programmable floor robots and videos (Activity 4).

- **Health and safety**: children under 12 months must not eat honey. Check allergies before starting Activity 1.

- **Key vocabulary**: forwards/backwards, waggle, spin, measure, mix, listen, healthy.

Steady

Before teaching, reflect on the following goals/learning intentions:

- To listen attentively in a range of situations.

- To show good control and coordination in small and large movements.

- To create simple programs.

- To make observations of animals and plants.

- To talk about ways to keep healthy and safe.

Go

Activity 1: Jam jar cookery

There are lots of simple and healthy non-cook dishes that can be prepared in a clean jam jar. These are easily transported home and can be eaten straight from the jar. How about trying overnight oats? There are many different recipes which involve minimal preparation and use non-standard measures, so they are ideal for young children. For instance, try a choc chip and banana version: add one-third of a cup of plain Greek yoghurt, half a cup of porridge oats, two-thirds of a cup of unsweetened milk of your choice, up to two tablespoons of honey or maple syrup (to taste), half a ripe banana (chopped or mashed) and two tablespoons of chocolate chips to a bowl, mix and add to jars. Leave in the fridge for at least four hours. As a snack in a jar, rocky road popcorn is a simple and comparatively healthy alternative to chocolate and sweets: either pop your own kernels or buy shop-bought sweet popcorn. Spread on a baking tray and drizzle with melted chocolate and allow to set. Mix with dried fruit, mini marshmallows, nuts and seeds and place in jars. Or for more indulgence, how about Eton mess: crumble meringue nests into the jar and add berries and whipped cream. Extend by planning, preparing and selling the jars in the school snack shop or at a school fair to develop enterprise skills.

Activity 2: Honey bee dance

Bees are amazing creatures. When they find a source of food they communicate its location to other bees in the hive through complex dances. There are examples of this on YouTube (e.g. https://www.youtube.com/watch?v=-LA1OTMCJrT8), although these examples may not be suitable for the youngest learners. In the hall, introduce the children to key moves such as spins, turns, tail waggles and forwards and backwards steps. With a partner, encourage them to plan a sequence of perhaps five moves. They can record this sequence on large paper, then practise, refine and perform their own honey bee dance.

Activity 3: Flight of the Bumblebee

Nikolai Rimsky-Korsakov wrote the musical piece 'Flight of the Bumblebee' about a prince who is turned into a bee. Start by talking about how bees move and sound. Can the children use their fingers to make curvy paths, starting high or low, and buzz as they do this? Now listen to the piece of music. How does it make them feel? Can they hear the buzzing? Listen again, and this time ask the children to draw the sound of the music thinking about fast/slow, high/low, loud/quiet, considering what kind of movement the music is trying to represent. Extend by giving the children ribbons and allowing them to move in time to the music, before performing their flight to their friends.

Activity 4: Programming a Bee-Bot (or other floor robot)

Talk about technology the children have used at school or at home. Introduce the Bee-Bot and tell the children that, in pairs, their task is to find out as many things about the Bee-Bot as they can:

◾ What does it do?

◾ How might it work?

◾ What does each button do? Can they tell a partner?

They could then work in pairs to create a short video to explain what each button does on the Bee-Bot. Once the children are familiar with the buttons then they can be set simple challenges – for example, can you build a home for Bee-Bot? Can you program Bee-Bot to enter its home and leave without knocking the bricks over? Extend by creating a bee dance program for the Bee-Bot to perform.

Other ideas

◾ **Growing crystals**: substances such as salt and sugar are made up of tiny crystals. Children can be excited to grow their own crystals in a jam jar, although this activity needs to be adult led. Avoid getting washing soda on the skin. You need a clean jar, washing soda (or Epsom salts), a piece of cotton thread, a pencil, a paper clip and some hot water. Pour hot water into the jar (place a metal spoon in the jar to prevent the jar cracking). Put two or three teaspoons of washing soda into the jar and stir until dissolved. Repeat until no more soda will dissolve.
Tie the paperclip to the thread, and wrap the rest of the thread around the pencil. Drop the clip into the jar and place the pencil over the top of

the jar so the clip is suspended in the solution. As the water cools crystals will form on the paperclip, and after a few days these will slowly cluster together. Explore using poster paint in the water to create coloured crystals, or shape pipe cleaners instead of the paperclip to create different designs.

■ **Growing beans**: select four large dried beans or seeds – such as runner beans or chickpeas. Soak them in water for several hours. Fill a jam jar with a paper towel wrapped in a coloured serviette (this is just for decoration!). Place the beans around the edge of the jar, between the glass and the paper. Add enough water to make the serviette wet and leave in a sunny place. After a few days, the beans should start to sprout and the children can look closely at the roots that are forming. After a fortnight, there should be a beanstalk big enough and strong enough to plant outside.

Find out more

■ Find out more facts about bees at: https://matteroftrust. org/4754/20-amazing-honey-bee-facts.

■ There are several simple Bee-Bot activities available at: https://www. edex.com.au/downloads/dl/file/id/247.

K is for Kites

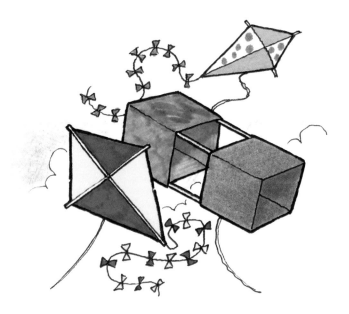

In a nutshell

The kite is the earliest form of aircraft created by humans. The Chinese invented kites more than 2,000 years ago. One legend is that the idea originated with a Chinese farmer who tied a string to his hat to keep it from blowing away in strong winds. The earliest kite frames were constructed from bamboo and covered with silk and paper.

Kites have been used in wars for target practice and to send signals, measure distances, drop letters and lift people. They have also been used for research. In 1899, the Wright brothers used kites when experimenting with the first airplane. In the 1950s, kites were also used to help in spaceship recovery missions.

Kites only became popular as toys in Victorian times. The development of new materials such as nylon, fibreglass and carbon graphite have made kites lighter, brighter and stronger. Kite sports such as kiteboarding, kite-surfing and kitebuggying are attracting growing interest, especially among young people. Kiteboarding featured in the 2018 Youth Olympic Games.

The Chinese are recognised as world experts in kite making and flying. Kite construction involves three stages: framing, gluing and decorating. Frames are put together using light wood such as bamboo. Kite makers often base their design on birds, butterflies, dragonflies and dragons. The kite's 'sail' can be made from silk, paper or nylon. Modern materials, such as nylon and plastic, allow for more colour and some designs include LED lights and sound.

Did you know?

- Kites were flown even before paper was invented. They were made from leaves.

- In 1752, Benjamin Franklin and his son William used a kite to prove that lightning was indeed electricity.

- In 2014, the largest kite in the world was flown in China and measured 110 metres long and 15 metres wide and weighed 200 kilograms.

- The smallest kite in the world, which flies, is 5 mm high.

- Kite-flying teams perform aerial ballets using a combination of kites.

- Kite fighting is popular in China and some other Asian countries.

- Kites have been used to smuggle goods across borders.

- Kites were once used to train falcons and hawks for hunting.

Ready

■ **Key resources**: paintings such as *The Kite* by John Morgan, interactive whiteboard (Activity 1); paper, tissue paper, straws, sticky tape, string, thread or yarn, pictures of Chinese kites (Activity 2); plastic bottle, plastic bag, decorations, sticky tape, string (Activity 3); a range of materials for making wind chimes, string (Activity 4).

■ **Health and safety**: ensure children have appropriate clothing for outdoor activities, and make sure that care is taken on windy days. Activity 3 will need adult supervision to cut and use plastic bottles and bags.

■ **Key vocabulary**: flying, floating, heavy/light, same/different, stick, fix, best, together, edge.

Steady

Before teaching, reflect on the following goals/learning intentions:

■ To develop narratives and explanations by connecting ideas or events.

■ To show good control and coordination in large and small activities.

■ To use and explore a variety of materials, tools and techniques, experimenting with colour, design, texture, form and function.

Go

Activity 1: Zoom in on *The Kite*

Choose a famous painting such as *The Kite* by the British artist John Morgan. Using the interactive whiteboard reveal a small part of the painting at a time. Can the children describe what they see? Can they make inferences about what the picture might be about using their observations to help them? Encourage the children to pay close attention to detail and to use appropriate vocabulary to describe what they see. Once the whole painting is revealed, talk to the children about when and where it was painted, and what the story of the main characters might be. Do they think it was painted a long time ago or recently? Why?

Activity 2: Chinese kites

A simple kite can be made by cutting a diamond kite shape from paper decorated with the children's own designs. There are lots of images and examples available online for inspiration. Start by taping two straws across the back of the paper in a cross pattern. These should run horizontally across the widest part of the kite and lengthways down the middle. Thread string through the two straws and knot together, then attach a length of string (as long as needed for flying) to the knot. Tape some long lengths of tissue paper to the bottom of the kite and test in the wind.

Activity 3: Windsock

A windsock can help tell where the wind is coming from and how strong it is. Use a plastic bottle with the bottom and top cut off to make the cylindrical frame. At one end of the cylinder pierce two holes and thread string through these to make the handle. Now make a tube shape from a plastic bag and tape to the other end of the cylinder, leaving the ends open so the wind can pass through. The children can decorate these with colourful bits of fabric, paper or plastic, adding long ribbons to fly in the wind.

Activity 4: Wind chimes

Collect some metal cutlery, old keys, natural materials such as sticks and recycled materials like small plastic bottles. Explore the sounds these make as they bang gently against one another. Invite the children to consider ways to attach these with string to branches or use simple wooden frames or coat hangers as the base of their wind chime. Attach the objects – for example, by threading them onto string or by tying and knotting – then hang in the wind and listen to the sounds that are made. Talk about the sounds and ask the children to choose their favourite ones.

Younger children could thread beads, cubes or bottle tops onto string and attach this to upturned plastic drinking cups for a simple indoor version.

Other ideas

■ **Stained-glass kites**: it may be too wet to fly a paper kite outdoors, so instead consider a beautiful display of stained-glass kites on your classroom windows. Cut out a kite shape from black construction paper and two more identical shapes from sticky-back book cover film. Then cut out the centre of the kite, leaving a 2 cm frame. Remove the backing from the sticky-back film and place the frame onto the sticky side. Now use a variety of coloured pieces of tissue paper to fill in the frame, sticking it to the sticky film as a collage. When finished, carefully cover with a second piece of sticky film and trim any overlaps. Add streamers for the tail.

■ **Toy parachutes**: make a toy parachute from a square of plastic or a cotton handkerchief. Throw the parachute into the air and watch what happens. Tie each corner of the square to a toy and then see how effective the parachute is. Do heavy or light toys come back to earth more quickly? Does a big or small square of parachute work best?

Find out more

■ STACK is an organisation that supports kite flying in the UK. Its website includes examples of spectacular kite ballet from around the world: http://www.savell.plus.com/stack/comp-ballet.html.

■ There are lots of websites which give ideas for parachute games for children – for example, for the early years see: http://www.earlyyearscareers.com/eyc/learning-and-development/top-5-parachute-games-children-early-years.

L is for Logs (and Leaves)

In a nutshell

Logs are part of a tree trunk or branch that has been cut down or fallen off. The systematic cutting down of trees (logging) has happened throughout history and all over the world. In the United States, logging has been big business for more than 400 years. Logs were needed to build ships, houses and, later, the railways. By the eighteenth century, much of England's forests had been exhausted in supplying ships for the navy.

The destruction of woodland remains a controversial issue. According to a 2015 article in *Nature*, it is estimated that we have lost 46% of the world's trees since civilisation began. However, organisations such as the Forestry Commission and the Woodland Trust (with its motto 'protect, restore and create') are helping to preserve the country's woodlands for the benefit of people and wildlife.

Many invertebrates live in and feed on rotting wood. These include beetles, millipedes, spiders, snails, worms and wasps. In the United Kingdom, woodpeckers, owls, bats, weasels, hedgehogs, squirrels and foxes are among the birds and mammals who nest in hollow trees and logs.

Leaves come in all shapes, sizes and textures. Most leaves are broad, flat and thin. This maximises the surface area directly exposed to sunlight and allows photosynthesis to occur. Leaves store food and water to support the plant's growth.

Did you know?

- In Japan, as part of the ancient Onbashira Festival that occurs every six years, men sit on a huge tree trunk and roll down a mountain. People are often injured or killed.

- NASA calculates that forests currently cover 30% of the Earth's land surface.

- NASA also estimates that within 100 years there will be no rainforests.

- A 2015 report in *Science* suggests that about fifty football pitches' worth of forest is cut down every minute.

- In Canada alone, a thousand new tree seedlings are planted each minute.

- The World Wildlife Fund calculates that global wood consumption could triple by 2050.

- The tallest trees in the world are in the Redwood National and State Parks in California. The coast redwood can grow to around 115.5 metres.

- Log flumes, now familiar because of theme park rides, started as a way to move logs using man-made troughs.

Ready

- **Key resources**: sticks, thread, natural resources such as leaves and feathers (Activity 1); leaves, plastic plates/bowls/cups, PVA glue, cling film (Activity 2); natural materials (Activities 3 and 4).

- **Health and safety**: remember to respect wild spaces and be considerate when collecting natural objects. Don't collect berries or fungi and supervise the use of tools. Ensure hand-washing hygiene.

- **Key vocabulary**: stick, hard/soft, dry/wet, feel, bend, colour, shape, smooth/bumpy, stalk, vein, bark, prickly/smooth.

Steady

Before teaching, reflect on the following goals/learning intentions:

- To be confident to try new activities.

- To investigate objects and materials.

- To find out about features of living things.

- To handle tools, objects and materials safely and with increasing control.

- To represent ideas, thoughts and feelings through design and technology, art and story.

Go

Activity 1: Journey sticks

Have the children ever forgotten something? Read stories such as *Mog the Forgetful Cat* by Judith Kerr (1972). Talk about how we try to remember things and share ideas that help us – for example, a birthday book, alarm or calendar. What could they use if they didn't have paper, pens or a mobile phone? Explain how First Nations people used to decorate a stick as a reminder of the places they had been and to help tell others about their journey. Show the class an example of a decorated stick and recite the journey this stick could tell. Explain that their task is to go on a journey in the school grounds and to make a stick to help them remember their journey. Encourage the children to choose objects such as leaves, grasses and feathers, and help them to explore how to bind them to their stick with wool and thread. Choose appropriate colours – for example, brown for a muddy puddle and blue for a pond. Allow them time to tell their friends the story of their journey using the stick to help.

Activity 2: Leaf plates and bowls

Autumn leaves are beautiful and can be used to create some wonderful objects. Ask the children to collect dry leaves of various shapes, sizes and colours. Talk about these and ask the children to sort them in different ways. Then take two identical plastic cups (or bowls or plates). Cover the outside of one in cling film (tape on the inside to hold firm, if needed). Arrange the leaves on the cling film, securing in place with PVA glue (add a little water to make it easier to work with). Continue to layer the leaves until the cling film is well covered. Place another piece of cling film over the top of the leaves, and then place on the matching cup and squash together. After drying for a day or two in a warm place, remove one of the cups and gently peel away the cling film. Check to ensure all the leaves are covered in glue, then remove the second cup and cling film to reveal a cup made from leaves.

Activity 3: Natural art gallery

Use a log as the basis for some 3D art. Encourage each child to mix and shape mud in their hands before pressing this onto a log and shaping it into a face, or ask them to work together to create a whole creature. Decorate with natural materials. Name the creations – for example, mudosaurus, the mud dinosaur. Tell stories about the creature – is it friendly, mischievous or scary?

Activity 4: Giant nest

Talk about where woodland creatures sleep. What sort of places do they feel safe in? In the outdoor classroom, can the children create a cosy, comfy nest big enough for two people? Encourage them to be creative and solve design problems as they arise. They should choose a suitable space, pick up lots of sticks in different shapes and sizes and add soft dry grass and feathers to sit on.

Other ideas

- **Camouflage masks**: make card or papier-mâché masks in the shape of woodland creatures. Collect natural resources like leaves, twigs and grasses to decorate the masks and talk about how and why animals use their fur, feathers and skin to blend into their surroundings.

- **More than just a stick**: encourage the children to think of different uses for a stick. Read *Stanley's Stick* by John Hegley (2011). Stanley's stick is not just a stick; he uses it to help him fly to the moon, to write in the sand and much, much more.

- **Leaf snap**: collect two of a variety of leaves of different colours, shapes and sizes and use them to play a game of 'snap', practising matching and sorting skills.

- **Sawing, carving, hammering and drilling**: old logs offer an exciting chance for children to use real tools (under adult supervision), developing a range of fine motor skills.

- **Mark-making magic**: using some mud or modelling clay, let the children explore using natural objects such as acorns, sticks and pine cones to make marks. Encourage them to roll, press and so on to see what sort of different marks they can make.

Find out more

■ The Woodland Trust website has hundreds of ideas using wood for activities for children of all ages: http://www.woodlandtrust.org.uk/naturedetectives.

■ Andy Goldsworthy creates beautiful natural artwork. Find out about this at: https://www.bbc.co.uk/education/clips/zh4wmp3. Use his work as an inspiration for your own natural art gallery.

M is for Maps

In a nutshell

The oldest known map of the world dates to around 600 BC. It was created by the Babylonians on clay and shows Babylon as the centre of the world, along with mountains and lakes. The ancient Greeks, Chinese and Romans made more detailed maps.

The first maps were painted by hand on parchment made from animal skins. This made it difficult to draw exactly the same map over and over again. Things improved with the invention of the printing press, which made it possible to mass-produce maps.

The first ever road atlas of Britain was published in 1675 by John Ogilby. It showed seventy-three major roads; there are now over 250,000 roads. In 1747, King George II ordered a survey of the Scottish Highlands while fighting the Jacobites. This led to the development of Ordnance Survey maps, particularly from the 1840s. Today, Ordnance Survey is one of the world's largest producers of maps.

Modern mapping software such as Google Street View allows users to pick a point on a map and view the location as if they were standing in the street. The photographs are electronically 'glued' together to make a seamless view of the location.

Did you know?

■ Cartography is the study of maps and map making. Someone who makes maps is called a cartographer.

■ North is at the top of modern maps, but during the Middle Ages most maps put east at the top. In Latin, the word for east is *oriens*, and to hold a map correctly you had to 'orient' it – to make sure east was at the top. This is where the word 'orientation' comes from.

■ In 2003, the US Library of Congress paid a record US$10 million for a German map printed in 1507 – it was the first map to include America.

■ Early map makers in the United States included fake towns to catch forgers when they tried to sell maps which they had copied.

Ready

■ **Key resources**: maps, atlases, aerial photos from Google Maps.

■ **Health and safety**: if using maps as part of a local walkabout, ensure that the children are reminded of road safety rules.

■ **Key vocabulary**: above/below, aerial view, north, south, east, west, perspective, map, satellite, place, cartographer, atlas, locality, orientation.

Steady

Before teaching, reflect on the following goals/learning intentions:

■ To follow simple directions using positional language.

■ To identify local physical features using aerial photographs.

■ To compare different maps and identify similarities and differences.

Go

Activity 1: Map of the classroom

Show the children a simple map of the classroom and introduce words to describe the location of things (e.g. the books are next to the window). Model the drawing of a simple signpost map showing the location of objects in relation to yourself: things that are closest, things that are nearby and things that are far away. Ask the children to create and explain their own signpost map using locational vocabulary (e.g. the computers are nearer to me than the hall).

Extend this by asking the children to draw their home on the map and, in another lesson, a map of their journey from home to school.

Activity 2: High above

Use Google Maps (satellite view) to explore an aerial view of the school and identify key features (e.g. rivers, ponds, parks, roads, railway lines, buildings).

Discuss why aerial views are useful and who might use them (e.g. police helicopter/search and rescue pilots). Explain how maps are a simple representation of an aerial view; they help us to understand where things are located.

Activity 3: Maps, maps, maps

Provide the class with a range of maps on different scales to explore (e.g. a map of the world and a map of the locality). Ask the children to think about things they have in common, such as titles, labels, symbols and so on. Discuss with the children what information they find on the maps. Explain that maps tell us where places are – that is, their location. Show the children some poor examples of maps that do not have adequate information (these can be sketched and prepared yourself) and discuss why they are not good maps. Create an ongoing checklist of things the children find out that maps should have, and ensure this is accessible to them. Develop mapping experiences further by exploring a simple map of the immediate area. Ask the children to identify the school, the roads surrounding it, places of interest and so on. Discuss the symbols used on maps and find out what they represent by using the key.

Other ideas

- **Treasure maps**: create a role play area linked to the theme of pirates. Involve the children in designing and making the ship, masts, telescopes, costumes, jewellery, treasure chests, coins, flags and treasure maps.

- **Treasure hunt**: plan a treasure hunt around the school. Provide clues and encourage the children to use vocabulary related to the map.

- **Direct an adult**: ask a learning support assistant to play the part of a robot and get the children to direct his or her movements around the hall or playground using directional language (e.g. left, right, forward three steps, backward one step). This is a useful introduction to Activity 4 under 'J'.

Find out more

■ Digimap allows teachers to access maps and aerial photographs of the UK for a small annual fee: http://digimap.edina.ac.uk.

■ The Geographical Association is the main professional body for teaching geography and has many resources on its website: www.geography. org.uk.

■ The Royal Geographical Society has some Key Stage 2 resources that can be adapted for younger children: www.rgs.org.

N is for Notebooks

In a nutshell

The ancient Egyptians and Sumerians were the first to use paper for writing, followed by the Chinese. Over the centuries, most paper for notebooks was derived from trees, although it has also been made from rice, plants, cotton and even clothes. Most of the paper in today's notebooks comes from a mixture of wood pulp and recycled paper.

Very famous people such as Ludwig van Beethoven, Charles Darwin, Thomas Edison and Albert Einstein kept notebooks. Leonardo da Vinci, the great Renaissance artist, was left handed and his notebooks are famous for being written in mirror script, from right to left. Perhaps this was to avoid smudging the paper. He recorded amazing ideas such as flying machines and diving suits.

In 1989, the first A4-sized computer appeared. The NEC UltraLite was dubbed by journalists as a 'notebook' to distinguish it from the heavier computers around at the time. However, writing by hand using notebooks is coming back into fashion. Today, notebooks come in all shapes and sizes.

Did you know?

■ The word paper comes from papyrus, a plant which once grew in abundance in ancient Egypt.

■ Leonardo da Vinci's notebooks contain 13,000 pages.

■ In 1770, Englishman John Tetlow invented a machine to produce lined paper.

■ In 1997, Maria Sebregondi trademarked the Moleskine brand of high quality stationery. The famous luxury notebooks are inspired by Bruce Chatwin's descriptions of the beautiful bound notebooks which were sold in Paris during the nineteenth and twentieth centuries.

■ The largest notebook in the world is 0.99 m².

Ready

■ **Key resources**: roll of plain wallpaper/backing paper, varied writing materials (Activity 1); natural materials such as mud, berries, leaves, flowers and ash, pestle and mortar (or homemade equivalent), paper (Activity 2); old magazines, comics, greetings cards, etc. with animal images on them, scissors, glue, pens and paper (Activity 3); a child's tool belt, special stationery (Activity 4).

■ **Health and safety**: take care when on the move with pencils or pens in hands, and remind the children not to eat any wild materials they find. Encourage good hygiene through hand washing, especially after Activities 2 and 3.

■ **Key vocabulary**: stir, crush, pound, write, note, idea, next, before/after.

Steady

Before teaching, reflect on the following goals/learning intentions:

■ To use phonic knowledge to write words in ways which match their spoken sounds.

■ To write simple sentences which can be read by themselves and others.

■ To choose resources needed for activities.

■ To write for a variety of purposes and audiences.

Go

Activity 1: Never-ending notebook

Source a long roll of plain wallpaper. Place this somewhere where it can be unrolled a little at a time – perhaps in a corner of the classroom. Start a story with the children and encourage them to add what happens next. Provide a varied range of mark-making equipment to engage the children. When they have added an element to the story, they can invite a friend to add the next part, using marks, words, pictures or symbols. Can they tell you the story so far? Alternatively, pre-populate the never-ending notebook with interesting words, images or photos and allow the children to unroll a little at a time and add comments or pictures of their own.

Activity 2: Nature's notebook

Early artists, such as the cave painters in Lascaux, France, used natural resources to create their artwork. Encourage the children to explore natural materials and to make marks with the resulting 'inks'. Explore the range of colours that could be made and ask the children to make predictions about shades and colours. Use ash or charcoal for black, blackberries or blueberries for purples and blues, mud for brown and leaves and grasses for green. Experiment to see what happens if the materials are mixed or if water is added. The children could write messages to their friends using the natural inks.

Activity 3: Mix 'n' match notebook

Obtain a large notebook or scrapbook and place it in the creative area. Provide the children with a range of animal pictures from magazines, greetings cards, old books, etc. Get them to cut these out and create new and fantastic animals by sticking one head to a different body. Extend by providing starting features and asking the children to draw in additional parts of the body. What would they call their new animal? What does it like to do? What does it like to eat? Where does it live? Although intended for seven- to nine-year-olds, Ricky Gervais's 2004 book *Flanimals* (and others in the series, including the pop-up book) may provide inspiration and contains wonderful names such as 'Mernimbler' and 'Munty Flumple' to get you started.

Activity 4: Go anywhere notebook (and writing belt)

You will need to source or make a tool belt for this activity, and then fill it with special stationery – beautiful pens and pencils, some with glitter and sparkle, scented pens, thick pencils and so on. Place a special notebook or two inside the belt as well. This then becomes the 'go anywhere' writing toolkit – meaning the children can make marks throughout your setting whenever they feel that they need to make a note of something important. This might be to remember seeing a ladybird on a leaf, to jot down how many friends are choosing the scooters or to record what resources are needed in the construction area. This helps the children to see writing as a valuable skill, rather than something they only do in the writing area.

Other ideas

■ **Cloud watching**: clouds come in some amazing shapes and sizes, and often resemble animals or objects. Read a book such as *Shapes in the Sky* by Josepha Sherman (2004). Place a cloud-shaped notebook in the outdoor space on a cloudy day. Encourage the children to become 'cloud detectives' and make careful observations about clouds in the notebook, noting shape, size and when it was seen. Was it a fast or slow moving cloud? What does it remind them of? Remind the children not to look directly at the sun.

■ **Doodle designs**: in a sketchbook, create some doodles that include wavy lines, straight lines and so on. Encourage the children to look closely at the doodles and add to them to create their own works of art. They can explore shape, line, colour, shading, letters and so on. Books like *The Usborne Doodle Pad* by Kirstene Robson (2012) and activity packs like *Animal Doodles* by Fiona Watt (2010) can provide lots of ideas for doodle notebooks.

Find out more

■ The Literacy Shed website has lots of exciting starting points for engaging young writers and readers: www.literacyshed.com.

■ Arrange for a real-life author to come to talk to your children and get them inspired to read and write. The Book Trust has a useful website: https://www.booktrust.org.uk/supporting-you/practitioners/how-to-arrange-an-author-visit.

■ Go on a walk in your local area and look for people who write things down in real life – maybe in a cafe, shop or business. Encourage the children to look carefully at where and how the individuals use writing to help them.

O is for Oatmeal

In a nutshell

In the UK we usually refer to oatmeal as porridge. Porridge is made from a cereal, usually oats boiled in water or milk. For thousands of years it has been part of the great British breakfast. In Scotland, families had 'porridge drawers' where porridge or 'porage' was stored to solidify and then eaten later as solid oat bars.

Scotland has lots of porridge traditions – for example, porridge should always be served in a wooden bowl and be eaten standing up. This is perhaps because in the past rural workers did not have much time for breakfast.

In 1877, Quaker Oats registered the first trademark for a breakfast cereal. Today the company sells a wide range of oat products including muesli, granola and a Fruit and Oat Squeeze drink.

Studies show that porridge is a very healthy breakfast option – for example, *Nutrition Reviews* reported that one particular fibre found only in oats (called beta-glucan) lowers cholesterol which can help to protect against heart disease. However, this only refers to the natural oatmeal. Sachets of instant porridge contain high levels of sugar and salt. According to *The Independent*, one pot of golden syrup flavour Quaker Oat So Simple porridge contains over four teaspoons of sugar!

Did you know?

■ World Porridge Day (which is organised by the charity Mary's Meals) takes place on 10 October to raise money for starving children.

■ The man who features on the Quaker Oats box is not an actual person. He is dressed to look like a Quaker, a member of a Christian faith group who are associated with the values of integrity, honesty and purity.

■ Since the 1950s, the expression 'doing porridge' has been used as slang for being in prison and refers to prison breakfast.

■ The first person to record the story of Goldilocks and the Three Bears was the Poet Laureate Robert Southey in 1837.

■ In 2003, an undercover reporter posing as a footman revealed that the Queen's breakfast table is laid out with cornflakes and porridge oats in Tupperware containers, yoghurt and two kinds of marmalade.

Ready

- **Key resources**: porridge oats, water, milk, syrup and other toppings, a range of fruits (such as berries), bowls, spoons, cooker/microwave (Activity 1); the story of Goldilocks and the Three Bears (Activity 2); teddy bear, classroom photos with the bear (Activity 3); a collection of teddy bears (Activity 4).

- **Health and safety**: check allergies before cooking and tasting porridge recipes. Wash hands before preparing food.

- **Key vocabulary**: mix, stir, taste, add, behaviour, advice, over/under, around, left/right, next to, behind/in front of.

Steady

Before teaching, reflect on the following goals/learning intentions:

- To explore traditional tales.

- To consider alternative viewpoints and talk about behaviour and its consequences.

- To use everyday language to discuss size, weight and position.

- To know the importance of a healthy diet.

Go

Activity 1: Whose porridge is this?

Encourage the children to talk about foods they enjoy for breakfast. Have they tried porridge? Make a simple bowl of porridge and talk about the ingredients, the process and how it changes when it is cooked. Get the children to sequence the events in the process or write simple instructions. Research some tasty porridge recipes and provide a range of foods to add – for example, berries, banana, syrup, peanut butter, milk and sugar. Explore different tools – for example, grate some apple, chop the banana and talk about measuring. Carry out taste tests and see which is the most popular porridge recipe in the class. Invite teachers, parents and children to send in photos of their favourite porridge creations and guess who they belong to.

Activity 2: Give Goldilocks some advice

Tell the story of Goldilocks up to the point where she eats the porridge. Ask the children to talk about why Goldilocks might have decided to eat the porridge. How do they think she felt? Ask the children to stand in two lines facing one another. This is the 'conscience alley'. Give a child at one end a teddy bear – when they have the bear they can speak. Pretend to be Goldilocks and move slowly down the line, talking to the children. Ask them to describe to Goldilocks how the bears might feel when they get home. For those who find explaining their thinking difficult, encourage them to show how they feel – for example, maybe they can show a sad face or perhaps they are angry with Goldilocks. Get them to talk about what Goldilocks could do to make the bears feel better.

Activity 3: Where are the bears?

Take photos of a teddy bear in different places in your provision – such as under a chair, behind the computers or in front of the board. Print out the pictures and place them in a small box. The children should work in pairs – one child has the box of photos and the other has the teddy bear. The child with the photos chooses a picture and describes it carefully to their partner. Can their partner listen carefully to the clues and put the teddy in the right place? For inspiration, the book *Where is Marmaduke?* by Karen Bryant-Mole (1998) has a teddy hiding in lots of different places.

Activity 4: Order the bears

Collect some different teddy bears. Get the children to work together to put them into order from tallest to shortest. How will they measure and compare the bears? Can they record their findings using ICT or a picture? Can they sort the bears into different groups? Can their friend guess the criteria they have used (e.g. colour, size, clothes)? Can they choose two bears that have something in common? Can their friend guess the connection between the two?

Other ideas

■ **Guess who's coming for dinner**: set up the role play corner ready for a dinner party or picnic for some bears. Decide how many are coming and ask the children to write invitations, plan a menu and lay the table. Can they set out the correct numbers of plates, bowls and so on? They could prepare some food such as sandwiches and fairy cakes. Extend by adding different requirements – for example, Mr Teddy only likes square sandwiches, while Miss Teddy likes triangular ones – or by researching what real bears would eat in the wild.

■ **Orange, Pear, Apple, Bear**: Read *Orange, Pear, Apple, Bear* by Emily Gravett (2011), which is a beautifully illustrated book containing just five words – 'orange', 'pear', 'apple', 'bear' and 'there'. Throughout the book these words are used in different ways – for example, on one page a brown bear juggles an apple, an orange and a pear, while on another there is an orange bear and on another a pear-shaped bear. Use this to talk about simple rhyme and word play. Perhaps you can create a new version using different characters – how about 'purple', 'fig', 'strawberry', 'pig' or 'red', 'grape', 'green', 'ape'?

Find out more

■ There are so many books about bears! Turn your reading corner into a bear's den and fill it with pictures, toys and books about these amazing creatures. Try Michael Bond's Paddington books such as *A Bear Called Paddington* (1958), A. A. Milne's Winnie the Pooh stories, Eric Carle's *Brown Bear Treasury* (2015), Mick Inkpen's *One Bear at Bedtime* (1987) or, of course, Michael Rosen's *We're Going on a Bear Hunt* (1989). Include some non-fiction choices like Terry Mason's *Bears!* (2017) as well.

■ There are several charities which work to protect bears in the wild. Find out more about their work and consider adopting your own school bear – for example: https://www.wwf.org.uk/wildlife/polar-bears

https://shop.chesterzoo.org/adoptions/select.aspx

https://give.bornfree.org.uk/adopt/bear.

P is for Pegs

In a nutshell

Pegs are short pins, usually tapered at one end, for holding things in place. Different types of pegs are used for different purposes. Tent pegs were used by ancient nomadic peoples, including the Hebrews, and are mentioned in the Bible. Survey pegs are used by surveyors on construction sites to establish boundaries and to take measurements. Carpenters have traditionally used wooden pegs to secure joints.

The everyday clothes peg was not invented until the nineteenth century. One suggestion is that fishermen invented the peg to clip their nets to the rigging. Before then, people just spread clothes out on the ground or on hedges or hung them over a line to dry (this type of washing line appears in a mural in the ancient city of Pompeii).

Traditional wooden pegs in Britain are made from willow and hazel. Gypsies were among Britain's early peg makers. They worked in the woodlands and sold their pegs in cities and towns. Shopkeepers would often pay them in goods rather than cash.

In the Second World War, when money was tight and toy making stopped, people made toys from any items they found inside and outside the home, including wooden clothes peg dolls.

Did you know?

■ In the Bible (Judges 4:21), it is said that Sisera, an enemy of the Israelites, was killed by a tent peg.

■ In 2009, a new world record was set for holding forty pegs in one hand.

■ The origin of the saying 'bring someone down a peg or two' is uncertain. One suggestion is that it relates to when people shared a drinking vessel called a 'pigin'. When this was passed around, each person drank down to their mark or peg. Anyone who upset the crowd had to miss a few turns and so was brought down a 'peg or two'.

■ In 2012, the largest clothes peg in history was unveiled in Germany – it measured 3.5 metres long, 65 cm high and 44 cm deep.

Ready

■ **Key resources**: Martin Waddell's *The Toymaker* (1993) (Activity 1); old-fashioned wooden pegs, pipe cleaners, felt-tip pens, pencils, glue, scissors, wool, bits of fabric and felt, beads, buttons, ribbons, lace and other haberdashery items (Activity 2); wooden pegs and washing line (Activity 3).

■ **Health and safety**: remind the children about the safe use of tools and materials.

■ **Key vocabulary**: doll, peg, wooden, plastic, old/new, change, difference.

Steady

Before teaching, reflect on the following goals/learning intentions:

■ To talk about past and present in children's lives and their family members' lives.

■ To enable children to experiment with their own ideas through art and design and technology.

■ To sequence objects correctly.

Go

Activity 1: *The Toymaker*

Read Martin Waddell's story, *The Toymaker* (1993) in which Mary yearns to play with the children outside her father's toy shop but is too sick to do so. Her father decides to make three dolls that look like the children outdoors. Many years later, Mary and her granddaughter return to the toy shop and discover that her father's gifts survive. Use the story as a starting point to discuss old and new toys and encourage children to ask older relatives about their favourite toys when they were young.

Activity 2: Making peg dolls

Give the children some wooden pegs and haberdashery items and ask them to make an old-fashioned wooden doll to look like themselves. Chertsey Museum has full instructions on how to make a peg doll: http://chertseymu-seum.org/domains/chertseymuseum.org.uk/local/media/images/medium/Resources_For_..._Victorian_Toys.pdf.

Activity 3: Washing lines

Pegs on washing lines can be used for a wide range of activities (see 'S') – for example, order numerical birthday cards, sequence days of the week, display the instructions to make a sandwich or letters of the alphabet. Wooden pegs can be decorated with numbers and pegged in order or the children can attach the right number of pegs to number cards.

Other ideas

- **Produce a rainbow of coloured pegs and hang them on a washing line in the classroom**: how many colours can the children identify?

- **Make a learning line using pegs to hang up examples of work for each child to show how they have progressed through the term**: can the children remember doing the work? What can they do now that they couldn't do then?

Find out more

- Share with the class inventors and designers who have created new uses for traditional pegs. Examples can be seen at: http://www. architectureartdesigns.com/38-creative-diy-ideas-you-can-do-with-wood-en-pegs. Draw on your own experiences around the home – for example, pegs to seal food bags, as toothbrush holders or bookmarks.

- Research peg/toy dolls around the world, such as Diwali celebration dolls.

- Try to arrange a visit to a museum of childhood which exhibits old toys such as the V&A Museum of Childhood (http://www.vam.ac.uk/moc) or use images from online collections – for example, the National Museum of Wales: https://museum.wales/traditional_toys/peg_dolls.

Q is for Queen's Head

In a nutshell

The monarch's head has appeared on lots of records in history. For example, the Great Seal, which included the monarch's profile, was stamped on documents to show the highest approval in the land.

Kings and queens wanted to create a good impression, hence coins, which featured their portraits, were carefully minted to convey messages of power, majesty and awe. Coins were, in fact, the very earliest form of propaganda. For centuries, coins were the only way ordinary people might see an image of their king or queen. Until the Tudors, coins bore no resemblance to how the monarch looked.

The monarch's head has appeared on British stamps since the Penny Black was introduced in 1840. The Royal Mail has undertaken this voluntarily and willingly, although it only became a legal requirement in 2011.

New coins showing the first portrait of Her Majesty were issued in 1953. This announced a new Elizabethan era of optimism following the Second World War. During her reign, coins have featured five different portraits of the monarch, the last in 2015.

Did you know?

■ The Queen faces right on coins but left on postage stamps.

■ There are strict laws on using the Queen's head in advertising – no alterations are allowed.

■ The Queen's Head is one of the most popular names for pubs in Britain.

■ To deter forgery, the Queen's face on the £1 coin contains an invisible pigment which can only be detected using ultraviolet light.

■ A few of the £1 coins released in 2017 were found with a defect that caused the inner section, which features the Queen's head, to fall out. They have been auctioned online for up to £5,000 each.

■ The small lettering around the outside of the £1 coin is made by special laser equipment that costs £500,000.

■ The Queen has only been photographed crying on a handful of occasions.

Ready

■ **Key resources**: real coins, small pots/bowls or old purses, paper and wax crayons (Activity 1); appropriate resources depending on the product (Activity 2); a variety of commemorative stamps and coins (or their images), craft materials (Activity 3); *The Jolly Postman* by Janet and Allan Ahlberg (1986), envelopes, letters, postcards, greeting cards (Activity 4).

■ **Health and safety**: wash coins before use and wash hands after touching them. Ensure coins are not put into mouths.

■ **Key vocabulary**: count, order, more/less, pence, change, send, receive, commemorate.

Steady

Before teaching, reflect on the following goals/learning intentions:

- To use everyday language to talk about money, to compare quantities and to solve problems.

- To count reliably with numbers from 1 to 20, place them in order and say which is one more or less.

- To represent their own ideas through design and technology, art and stories.

Go

Activity 1: Money, money, money

Place one coin of each denomination into separate bowls, small pots or old purses. Vary the coins depending on the age and stage of development – for example, use only 1p and 2p coins for younger children and up to the full range for older children. Explain that the contents of a till have got muddled up and they need to organise it. Give the children time to handle the coins, to sort and compare and to put them in the correct pots. Look for similarities and differences. Use wax crayons or soft pencils to make rubbings of the different coins. Use magnifying glasses to look closely at the markings. What do all the coins have in common? What are the differences? Are all 10p coins identical? How much money do they have altogether? Count in steps of appropriate sizes.

Activity 2: Mini enterprisers

Encourage the children to design a product to market and sell, perhaps at the school fair or at parents' evening. This may fit with a topic or theme they are learning about – for example, they could design and make bird feeders, healthy smoothies, chocolate covered fruit kebabs or cress heads. The children could carry out some market research – for example, into their favourite fruits. Use this information to plan the product, and then make and test a prototype. Use social media to advertise the product – for example, place a photo on the school Twitter or Facebook account. Make the product and sell it, giving the children a chance to use their financial skills (e.g. giving change, calculating totals) in a real-life context.

Activity 3: Designing coins and stamps

The design of coins and stamps often tells a story or celebrates key events. Look at sets of coins or stamps and consider the designs – for example, the 50p coins minted for the London 2012 Olympics, to celebrate Beatrix Potter's 150th anniversary or the 2018 alphabet 10p coins. The year 2016 saw stamps celebrating Mr Men and Little Misses as well as Beatrix Potter. Provide the children with large stamp or coin templates and ask them to design their own sets of commemorative stamps and coins using a range of decorative materials. Encourage the children to tell the story of their design.

Activity 4: *The Jolly Postman*

In Janet and Allan Ahlberg's book *The Jolly Postman* (1986), the postman delivers letters, cards and postcards to characters from well-loved traditional tales. Create a large book with different characters and encourage the children to compose letters to them. They could write an invitation to attend Cinderella's ball or write a note from the Big Bad Wolf to say he is sorry for blowing down the pigs' houses. Discuss how we need addresses so that the letters can be delivered and explore how we write our address. What could the addresses for the different characters be?

Other ideas

- **Sorting and matching money**: collect piggy banks of different sizes and shapes – charity shops and car boot sales are a great source for these. Label the various piggy banks with the coins they take (e.g. 1p piggy bank). Ask the children to sort a pile of mixed coins (or bury the treasure in the sand tray and allow them to find it) and post the right coins into the right piggies. Extend the activity by labelling the pigs with different amounts of money and see if the children can use the right coins to make up that total.

■ **Parcel force**: collect a range of boxes, tubs and tins of various shapes, sizes and weights. Get the children to wrap these in paper (which can be decorated by them using finger paints, printing, stamping, etc.). How big a piece of paper do they need? Can they fold the corners neatly? What shapes can they see? Estimate the weight of the different parcels and arrange in order. Use scales or balances to check. Create challenge by having the smallest parcels weigh the most.

■ **Post the letters**: create a washing line that looks like a row of houses and attach pegs labelled with numbers or letters. Label a series of envelopes with the appropriate letters or numbers and invite the children to 'deliver' them to the correct address.

Find out more

■ The Royal Mint has developed a range of materials for teachers (https://www.royalmint.com/aboutus/education). Although aimed at Key Stages 2 and 3, there are lots of ideas that could be adapted. The materials include flash cards and the stories underpinning some of the coins' designs. You can also visit the Royal Mint, which is based in Llantrisant, south Wales.

■ Invite a local post-person into class to talk to the children about how letters are delivered, or arrange a visit to the local post office to see how letters are sorted and sent.

R is for Rocks (and Pebbles)

In a nutshell

Rock is a natural substance composed of different minerals that have been fused together. Pebbles are stones worn smooth by the action of water.

There are three basic types of rock which are formed in different ways: igneous, sedimentary and metamorphic. Igneous rocks are volcanic and are made from molten material. Examples include basalt, granite and pumice. Not all rocks are old. If a volcano erupts and the magma cools, the igneous rocks may be just a few days old.

Sediment gets deposited over time, often as layers at the bottom of lakes and oceans, eventually forming sedimentary rocks. Examples include sandstone, flint and chalk.

Metamorphic rocks, such as marble and slate, are formed by extreme pressure over time. However, rocks can change forms through weathering and erosion.

Throughout history, humans have used rocks to make tools, weapons, walls and buildings. The famous Taj Mahal (meaning 'crown of palaces') was constructed out of white marble between 1631 and 1653. It stood as a final resting place for Mumtaz Mahal, the third wife of Mughal Emperor Shah Jahan.

Today, rocks are used in everything from homes (bricks made from clay) and washing machines (concrete for balance) to computers, airplanes and cars (metals and plastics).

Did you know?

- The word 'igneous' comes from the Latin word *ignis*, which means 'of fire'.

- A diamond is the hardest of the more than 3,000 minerals.

- Rocks aren't always solid. Sand and mud are rocks.

- The largest meteorite ever discovered weighed 66 tonnes and fell from the sky in prehistoric times. It was named Hoba after the African farm where it was found in 1920.

- The famous Mount Rushmore sculptures of US presidents are carved into the batholith's granite rock face. They were designed as a tourist attraction in the 1930s and took five years to complete, involving a sculptor and over 400 workers.

- People who study rocks are called petrologists.

- Millions of meteorites, or rocks from space, travel through the Earth's atmosphere each day. But most of these vaporise when encountering our atmosphere and leave a trail as a shooting star.

Ready

■ **Key resources**: samples of rocks (e.g. chalk, limestone, granite, sandstone, slate, marble), magnifying glasses (Activity 1); photographs/ video clips of fossils, plaster of Paris, disposable gloves and goggles, yoghurt pots (Activity 2).

■ **Health and safety**: prolonged or repeated direct skin contact with plaster of Paris may cause irritation and attempts at removal may cause abrasion. Wash off any splashes on the skin immediately. Ensure that the room is well ventilated.

■ **Key vocabulary**: igneous, sedimentary, metamorphic, petrologist, meteorite, man-made rocks, brick, tile, concrete.

Steady

Before teaching, reflect on the following goals/learning intentions:

■ To provide opportunities for systematic and careful observations.

■ To sort different kinds of rocks according to simple physical properties.

■ To express ideas using various materials.

Go

Activity 1: Rock and fossil museum

Collect different examples of rocks and pebbles and ask the children to sort these according to size, colour, shape and so on. They could write labels to accompany the display. Encourage the children to observe the rocks closely using magnifying glasses and to record what they see in annotated drawings. Ask the children to provide guided tours of their museum.

Activity 2: Make your own fossils

Show the children examples of fossils using photographs or video clips from the Internet. Discuss how fossils are formed and where they can be found. Demonstrate how to make a fossil one step at a time. Provide plaster of Paris in small amounts in yoghurt pots. For detailed guidance on making the fossils, follow the directions from a reputable source, such as the Eden Project: http://www.edenproject.com/learn/schools/lesson-plans/great-fossil-hunters.

Activity 3: Dinosaur egg hunt

Discuss with the class the connection between fossils and dinosaurs. Prepare a presentation beforehand (using an app like Morfo) or ask a relative or colleague unknown to the children to pretend to be a newsreader. Film them reading a bulletin for the class announcing that a precious dinosaur egg has gone missing and a reward has been issued. Any news of its whereabouts should be reported to the school and class teacher (yourself). Ask the children to start looking for clues as to the egg's location. Discuss how to care for the egg. Role play what happens when it hatches and take photographs to record the event. Design and make baby dinosaurs.

Other ideas

- **Find the lost pebbles**: bury pebbles numbered from 1 to 10 in sand. Ask the children to find and arrange them in order. Alternatively, label each pebble with a letter and ask the children to make simple three-letter words.

- **Pebble presents**: ask the children to paint pebbles as a present for their parents. They might paint their names, garden insects or fancy words. Lots of ideas can be found at: https://www.persil.com/uk/dirt-is-good/arts-crafts/painting-pebbles-with-children.html.

Find out more

- Use Dianna Hutts Aston's book *A Rock Is Lively* (2012) as a basis for further discussion on the variety of rocks – from dazzling blue lapis lazuli to volcanic snowflake obsidian.

■ Research life in rock pools – the hardy plants and animals that survive the harsh marine environment.

■ Find out more about lighthouses (e.g. Lizard Point, Cornwall or Bell Rock, off Dundee) and people such as Grace Darling who have saved sailors from shipwreck.

S is for Socks and Shoes

In a nutshell

The first shoes were probably made from bark, large leaves and grass tied under the foot with vines. Our prehistoric ancestors wore soft shoes made of wraparound leather, rather like sandals or moccasins.

Major changes in shoe design occurred during the Tudor and Stuart periods. Heels were introduced in the 1590s and the buckle added to fasten shoes in 1660. The famous diarist Samuel Pepys wrote, 'This day I began to put on buckles to my shoes' (22 January 1660). King Charles I enjoyed wearing flamboyant knee boots.

The twentieth century witnessed many different styles of shoes including: T-bar shoes (1920s), two-coloured shoes (1930s), utility styles (1940s), winkle-pickers and stiletto heels (1960s), platform soles (1970s) and LED trainers (1990s).

Northamptonshire is one of the most famous counties in the world for manufacturing shoes and boots. It has been doing so for more than 900 years. The county provided boots for the American War of Independence and over two-thirds of the 70 million pairs of footwear for the First World War. Among the people who have had their shoes made in Northamptonshire are Queen Elizabeth II, James Bond, Darth Vader and Jumbo the Elephant!

Did you know?

■ In the Middle Ages, the length of the toe was an indication of status. The king and his court had shoes with the largest toes.

■ Until the 1850s there was no difference between left and right shoes – all were made straight.

■ The word 'sneakers' originally referred to the first rubber-soled shoes produced in 1917, which enabled the wearer to 'sneak up' on someone without being heard.

■ Some sportswear companies such as Nike collect athletic shoes and recycle them into basketball courts, tennis courts and running tracks.

■ The largest shoe in the world (as of 2013) measures 6.40 metres x 2.39 metres and is 1.65 metres high.

Ready

■ **Key resources**: collection of clean old shoes, images of early shoes, wax crayons and paper (Activity 1); mixed pairs of socks, large dice, washing basket (Activity 2); small blocks, tape measures/rulers, paper, pencils or crayons (Activity 3); examples of different footprints (Activity 4).

■ **Health and safety**: wash hands after handling old shoes. Check with parents in advance, especially if you are going to be taking off shoes and socks.

■ **Key vocabulary**: old/new, change, difference, sandal, strap, boot, trainer, sneaker, long/short, measure, match, pair, pattern.

Steady

Before teaching, reflect on the following goals/learning intentions:

■ To follow instructions involving several ideas or actions.

■ To compare the similarities and differences between old and new shoes.

■ To sort, match and count familiar items (e.g. socks).

■ To use everyday language to talk about size and to compare quantities.

Go

Activity 1: Exploring old shoes

Ask parents and colleagues for old pairs of clean shoes of all sizes. Try to include more unusual examples such as ballet slippers or walking boots. Give the children the opportunity to play with these and try them on. Discuss what they have in common and sort according to criteria (e.g. colour, shape, weight, make, size, fastenings). Which shoes are the oldest and which are the most modern? How do they know? Show the children some pictures of very old shoes and compare them with those they have played with. Get them to make rubbings (using wax crayons and paper) of the soles of the shoes and talk about the patterns they see. Extend by deconstructing some of the shoes (i.e. to see how they are joined) or look at how the lights in flashing trainers work.

Activity 2: Hang out the washing

Place a washing basket with numerous pairs of socks mixed up in it on the carpet. Label a large blank dice with six colours, corresponding to the sock colours. Tip the socks out and look through them, talking about size, pattern and colour. Who might they belong to? Explain that the socks are all mixed up so the children need to play a game to sort them out. Let them take turns in rolling the dice. Can they find a sock with that colour on it and its matching pair? Extend by labelling a second dice with patterns such as spots, stripes, stars and so on to match the patterns in your sock collection. Can the children sort according to colour and pattern?

Activity 3: Comparing feet

Ask the children to stand on large sheets of paper and trace around their foot, or ask them to trace each other's feet. Get them to cut out the paper feet, helping them if needed. Discuss similarities and differences between each other's feet. Get the children to measure their feet using non-standard measures (such as blocks) or standard measures (such as centimetres), as appropriate. They could record the findings and then perhaps graph the results.

Activity 4: Footprints

Use the outdoor learning space, if possible, to place examples of different animal (or story characters – dinosaurs, etc.) footprints. Encourage the children to find and follow these and talk about what sort of animal might have made them. Where do they lead? Extend by researching or using a key to identify the animal. Leave some bird food in the middle of a tray of soft mud in a quiet corner of the playground and see if you collect any footprints during the day. Number large footprints and ask the children to order them.

Other ideas

- **Recycle old shoes**: these can be used as planters for bulbs, seeds and herbs. Old tights can be filled with soil, tied in a ball shape and placed in a small pot. Sprinkle grass seed on the top of the ball and water. The balls can be decorated as heads, and when the grass grows the children can cut the 'hair'.

- **Create a shoe shop in the role play area**: practise literacy and numeracy skills to buy and sell the shoes.

- **Wrap children's feet in bubble wrap**: stand in paint and create 'stomp' patterns on large pieces of paper, or step in muddy puddles and use the mud as paint. If you use 'clean' mud from a garden centre that has been checked, the children can have bare feet and enjoy the sensation of mud between their toes.

Find out more

- Read Tony Bradman's wonderful *The Sandal* (1989), which describes the story of a little Roman girl who loses her sandal in a river. It has gone forever … or has it? The book moves to the 1980s and a family's day out to a museum where they see the Roman sandal. On their way home, the little girl drops her sandal in the river. The final section of the story moves to AD 2250 and a family living out in space. A little girl's sandal is about to float off into space …

- Find out more about contributing to a shoe recycling charity. Talk to the children about how in some countries children do not have comfortable, well-fitting shoes, and discuss how your class could help. One initiative that schools can become involved with is https://www.clarks.co.uk/unicef.

- Linked to the theme of recycling, read Jane Cabrera's version of the classic *There Was an Old Woman Who Lived in a Shoe* (2017). This has a strong environmental message about repairing old furniture, shoes and clothes. Discuss with the class why this is important and where old boots and shoes can be recycled.

T is for Telephones

In a nutshell

The telephone is one of the most important inventions in history. Most people think Alexander Graham Bell invented the phone, but there are also claims for Elisha Gray and Antonio Meucci, an Italian inventor. The actual word 'telephone' was first used by Francois Sudré in 1828 for a musical signalling system.

British Telecom traces its history back to 1846, when it was called the Electric Telegraph Company. It was the first company to provide a national telephone service. The first phone book was issued in 1878 and was twenty pages long.

Mobile phone technology was first invented in the 1940s. But these early phones were little more than two-way radios that enabled people like taxi drivers and the emergency services to communicate. The 999 emergency number was introduced in 1937 following a fire in which five women were killed.

In 1973, Motorola produced the first handheld mobile phone, followed by firms such as Nokia (1997), Blackberry (1999) and Apple's iPhone (2007).

A poll conducted by Opinium Research in 2018 revealed that the average Briton spends 26 minutes a day checking their phone messages. The average adult receives ninety-three messages a day, although young people (aged 18–24) receive almost three times more messages and alerts a day (on average 239).

Figures published by the Ministry of Justice show that the use of mobile phones while driving has declined following the introduction of stiffer penalties in 2017. Mobile phone calls have saved lives and conveyed the most poignant messages, such as from those who lost their lives in the 9/11 terrorist attack.

Did you know?

- The first ever words spoken on the telephone were made on 19 March 1876 when Alexander Graham Bell said 'Mr Watson, come here – I want to see you.'

- Alexander Graham Bell recommended answering the telephone with the word, 'Ahoy-hoy'.

- In 1992, the first ever text message was sent in the UK. It said 'Merry Christmas'.

- In 2012, the world's longest telephone conversation took place in a Latvian shopping centre – it lasted 54 hours and 4 minutes.

- According to data from GSMA Intelligence, the number of mobile phones in the world overtook the number of people in 2014.

- The longest ever phone call in distance was between President Nixon and astronauts Neil Armstrong and Edwin 'Buzz' Aldrin while they were on the moon, on 20 July 1969.

- A Childwise Monitor report in 2018 found that 20% of five- to six-year-olds in the United States have their own mobile phone.

Ready

- **Key resources**: defunct mobile phones, pictures of old phones (Activity 1); pictures of emergency services, video clips of emergency calls (Activity 2).

- **Health and safety**: stress the importance of only ringing the emergency services in the event of a dangerous, serious or life-threatening situation.

- **Key vocabulary**: old/new, change/difference, telephone, mobile, conversation, emergency.

Steady

Before teaching, reflect on the following goals/learning intentions:

- To explore everyday technology in children's lives.

- To compare the similarities and differences between old and new phones.

- To know how to make an emergency phone call and when this may be necessary.

Go

Activity 1: Exploring old phones

Ask parents and colleagues for old mobile phones. Give the children an opportunity to play with these. Discuss what these have in common and sort according to criteria (e.g. colour, shape, weight, make, size). Which phone is the oldest and which is the most modern? How do they know? Show the children some pictures of very old phones, such as a candlestick phone, and ask them to compare these with the phones before them. Be mindful that some replica modern phones are often styled as older ones!

Activity 2: Help!

Show and discuss large pictures of a fire engine, ambulance and police car (and possibly coastguard helicopter depending on your location). When might we need to call these people? Introduce 999 – emergency (fire and rescue/police/ambulance/coastguard) – and stress that this number must only be called in a genuine emergency. Teach the children the importance of knowing their name, age and, if possible, location. Model scenarios that might call for different services. Stress that it is very unlikely they will need to make such a phone call, but it is good to be prepared. Share with the class real-life stories of children who have called the emergency services – for example, a two-year-old who rang when his mum collapsed (https://www.mirror.co.uk/news/uk-news/listen-amazing-boy-aged-2-4574757) and a three-year-old who rang when her pregnant mum was knocked out having fallen at home (https://www.mirror.co.uk/news/uk-news/listen-three-year-olds-incredible-7061392). Also share stories of calls that have wasted the precious time of emergency services (e.g. to remove nuisance seagulls).

Activity 3: Talk, talk, talk

Discuss with children the different kinds of conversations that can be had on the telephone – for example, to congratulate someone who has done well, to say sorry for upsetting a friend, to book an appointment, to say goodbye to someone who is moving away or to offer good/bad news. Ask the children to call a character in a story that you are reading. What will they ask them? What might the answers be?

Other ideas

■ **Ask the class who in the world they would most like to talk to on the phone**: pretend to be that person and hold the conversation.

■ **Create a string telephone**: there are lots of basic scientific ideas that can be developed. See suggestions at: http://www.sciencekids.co.nz/projects/stringphone.html.

■ **Show and discuss with the class video clips from the BT film archives**: these are available at: https://www.btplc.com/Thegroup/BTsHistory/BTfilmarchive/home/index.htm.

■ **Set up the role play corner as a telephone box**: encourage the children to go in and make phone calls to different people, and to take notes of important messages they might receive. Provide cards with different phone numbers on and the photo of who they belong to and encourage the children to press the corresponding numbers on the phone.

Find out more

■ Try to arrange a visit to a museum which has old telephones. A list can be found at: http://telephonesuk.co.uk/museums.htm.

■ Invite in a member of the emergency services (or visit a local fire station, etc.) to talk about how phones help them to do their jobs, and to reinforce the importance of only calling them in emergencies.

U is for Umbrellas

In a nutshell

Perhaps the origins of the umbrella began when prehistoric nomads carried a shelter of leaves around. Parasols (which are not waterproof) were first used by ancient peoples such as the Egyptians, Assyrians and Greeks more than 3,000 years ago. The Egyptian fashion was for pale skin and so the parasols protected them from the sun. The Chinese invented the waterproof umbrella using leather about a thousand years ago. From the sixteenth century, umbrellas started to become popular among wealthy European families. Elegant and fancy umbrellas were made for French women in the 1700s.

However, it was the traveller and writer Jonas Hanway who in the 1750s was the first Englishman to carry an umbrella regularly. Some English gentlemen still call their umbrella a 'Hanway'. Early umbrellas had wooden or whalebone handles and an oiled canvas covering. The pocket umbrella was invented in the 1920s.

Umbrellas are used for reasons other than keeping dry and protected from the sun. Some people have used umbrellas as plant covers, walking sticks, lampshades and even weapons. In the 1900s, women were instructed on how to fend off an attacker using an umbrella, while in the twentieth century umbrellas have been used in James Bond-style assassinations such as the murder of the journalist Georgi Markov in 1978.

Did you know?

■ The word 'umbrella' comes from the Latin root word *umbra*, meaning shade or shadow.

■ The word 'parasol' comes from the Italian *para* (protecting against) and *sole* (sun).

■ Umbrella hats were first made in 1880.

■ Most umbrellas are made in China. According to the *New Yorker*, the city of Shangyu alone has more than 1,000 umbrella factories.

■ In 2015, the National Federation of the Blind in the United States broke the world record for the largest umbrella mosaic. In total, 2,480 participants simultaneously raised umbrellas to create the image of the National Federation of the Blind icon, along with the organisation's tagline, 'Live the life you want'.

■ The largest umbrella in the world was made in the United Arab Emirates in 2018 and measures 24.5 metres in diameter and 15.22 metres in height.

■ In 2014, around 10,000 people were reported to have taken part in a traditional umbrella dance in China.

Ready

■ **Key resources**: range of umbrellas (Activity 1); samples of materials, such as bin bags, wool, denim, cotton, plastic beakers, small toys (Activity 2); recordings or video clips of songs about rain – for example, 'Singing in the Rain' (Activity 3).

■ **Health and safety**: model and remind children of how to put an umbrella up and take it down so that it does not poke anyone in the eye.

■ **Key vocabulary**: sort, match, umbrella, material, waterproof, predict.

Steady

Before teaching, reflect on the following goals/learning intentions:

■ To match and sort familiar objects.

■ To experiment with a variety of materials.

■ To sing songs and express feelings through dance and movement.

Go

Activity 1: Whose umbrella?

Create a story in which people have attended an event, such as a garden party, and have left their umbrellas in the cloakroom. Tell the children that all the umbrellas have been mixed up and they need to sort them out for the owners. How could these be categorised? Show the children a range of umbrellas (e.g. for a teenager, young child, golfer, football supporter) and ask them to work in small groups to look for clues and decide which umbrella belongs to which guest. Take care not to reinforce stereotypes!

Activity 2: Making your own umbrella

Discuss with the children what would make a good umbrella cover. They should consider waterproofing, strength, lightness, attractiveness and cost. Show the children some materials and ask them to predict which ones are likely to be waterproof (e.g. bin bag, wool, denim, cotton, net) and say why. How could they test these? How could they make the test fair? Put a toy inside a plastic beaker and cover it with the chosen material. Measure and pour a set amount of water over the material to see whether the toy gets wet or not. Discuss the results and how these might be presented. Consider extending to look at natural materials such as leaves.

Activity 3: Rainy day songs

Show children the classic clip of 'Singing in the Rain' featuring Gene Kelly from 1952. Set the children the challenge of singing songs and dancing in the rain and in muddy puddles. Examples can be found at: https://www.letsplaykidsmusic.com/rainy-day-nursery-rhymes and https://www.letsplay-kidsmusic.com/umbrella-song-rainy-day-songs. Extend to discuss other things that make them feel happy.

Other ideas

- **Create your own designer umbrellas**: bring into class some cheap single colour umbrellas. Cover the floor, open the umbrellas and then decorate them using waterproof fabric paint or pens. Let it dry for a day before closing or using.

- **Make a rain painting when light rain is forecast**: spread out a large sheet of paper before the rain begins, weighed down with heavy objects. Fill shaker dispensers with powdered paint. Sprinkle the paint randomly over the paper. The raindrops will mix and blend the paint. Bring in the wet painting and let it dry on layers of newspaper.

- **Have a raindrop race**: ask each child to pick a raindrop as it hits the classroom window and follow it to the bottom. Then choose again.

Find out more

- Read *Emily and the Rainbow Umbrella* by Maribeth Gabot and Lisl Fair (2012), which tells the story of Emily who wakes up one morning to find her birthday wish has come true and the whole world is pink, her favourite colour. The story celebrates the value of diversity and different colours.

- Research artists who have featured umbrellas in their work and discuss their techniques – for example, Renoir's *The Umbrellas* shows a bustling Paris street in the rain.

V is for Velcro (and Buttons and Zips)

In a nutshell

The ancient Indus civilisation made ornamental buttons out of seashells more than 4,000 years ago. Clothes fastened with buttons and button-holes have been around for about 700 years. By the 1900s, the zip fastener had been invented but only became popular once the US army started to use zippers.

Velcro is the brainchild of George de Mestral, a Swiss electrical engineer. In 1941, he went for a walk in the woods and noticed how burrs clung to his trousers and his dog. He wondered whether this could be turned into something useful. After seven years of research in the laboratory, de Mestral created a synthetic burr by using two strips of fabric, one with thousands of tiny hooks and the other with thousands of tiny loops.

After the 1960s, sales improved dramatically when Apollo astronauts successfully used it to stop pens, food packets and equipment floating away. In 1959, it was predicted that the new system would mark the end of buttons, hooks, zippers and safety pins. Velcro became part of our everyday lives in the 1980s when it was incorporated into the design of sports shoes by the likes of Puma, Adidas and Reebok.

Today, lots of the 'hook and loop' fasteners are made out of nylon, polyester and plastics. There are also options made from silver-coated steel, some of which are resistant to fire, and stretchy hook and loop fasteners, as is the case with fastenings for disposable nappies.

Did you know?

- In the 1930s, zip fasteners in children's clothes were advertised as a means of encouraging children to become more independent and sales increased.

- Velcro is the name of the company and trademark, not the invention, which is called 'hook and loop'. There are other hook and loop fastening systems, such as Scotch Extreme Fasteners.

- Velcro is a combination of two French words: *velour* (velvet) and *crochet* (hooks), so Velcro means 'velvet hooks'.

- A paper in *PLOS ONE* describes how one species of ant in French Guiana uses the Velcro principle by hanging onto the underside of leaves of the Cecropia tree (or trumpet tree) in large groups and waiting for insects to land. In return, the ants protect the host tree from defoliators (insects which strip the tree of its leaves).

Ready

■ **Key resources**: *Walter's Windy Washing Line* by Neil Griffiths (2008) (Activity 1); a range of clothing items with different fasteners (Activity 2); Velcro and magnifying glasses (Activity 3).

■ **Health and safety**: take care that fasteners such as buckles are not misused when handling different clothing items.

■ **Key vocabulary**: fastener, hook, button, zip, snap, buckle.

Steady

Before teaching, reflect on the following goals/learning intentions:

■ To listen attentively to a story and respond to what they hear with relevant comments, questions and ideas.

■ To investigate different materials using the senses.

■ To make observations and describe materials.

Go

Activity 1: Windy washing lines

Read *Walter's Windy Washing Line* by Neil Griffiths (2008) as a starting point for discussing different kinds of clothes and unexpected events. In the story, Walter is planning a nice weekend watching his favourite television pro-grammes, when a gust of wind blows his clothes from the washing line. Talk about times when the children have been out on a windy day. How did it feel? What happened? How did the wind sound? In the story, there are many opportunities to develop real-life mathematics – for example, using the tele-vision guide with times.

Activity 2: Wash basket

Collect and discuss a range of clothing items with different fasteners (e.g. hooks, buttons, zips, snaps, buckles). Put these in a box or basket and allow the children to explore them independently. Listen to what they say as they feel, use and wear the items. Discuss who might wear what, and sort, match and compare the items according to their fasteners.

Activity 3: How strong is Velcro?

Invite the class to carry out an experiment to see how strong hook fasteners can be. How much strength is needed to pull apart two strips of Velcro? Cut a length of 2–3 cm of Velcro and stick it to the lid of a plastic container. Pour 200 g of rice into the container. Screw the lid tightly onto the container and then weigh it. Ask the children to try to lift the container using the Velcro and record yes/no and the weight lifted. Try varying the weight of the rice to find out the maximum load. Does it matter if the container is lifted slowly? Discuss how to make the test fair (e.g. checking that the hook and loop strips overlap).

Other ideas

- **Close up**: use magnifying glasses to explore close-up what Velcro looks like. Can the children see the tiny hooks and loops? Ask them to draw a picture of the Velcro strips close up.

- **Carry out a survey of children's shoes in school**: find out what different fasteners are used and record the results using tally marks. Show on a pictogram or bar chart.

Find out more

- Find out more about how nature has inspired inventors. Visit websites such as https://cosmosmagazine.com/technology/10-technologies-inspired-nature to gain ideas to discuss with the class.

W is for Wellington Boots

In a nutshell

The wellington boot owes its name to Arthur Wellesley (1769–1852), 1st Duke of Wellington. He asked his shoemaker to improve upon the hessian army boots he wore. His new leather boots were lined with calfskin to ease the strain after a long day on the battlefield and to protect against gunshot wounds. The boot became popular among British gentlemen who wanted to imitate their hero. They wore wellington boots during hunting, fishing and other outdoor activities. In 1852, the boots began to be made from rubber rather than leather.

During both world wars, rubber boots were supplied to the soldiers. After the Second World War, wellington boots became popular among families.

Wellington boots are now sold in lots of different colours and styles including short, tall, warm, wedge, adjustable, sheepskin, slim calf, wide calf, steel toe capped and high fashion versions. Colours include choco-late, orange, pink, silver and violet, although green and black are the most popular in the UK.

Did you know?

■ The Duke of Wellington has more than ninety English pubs named after him.

■ The sport of wellie wanging involves throwing the boot as far as possible from a standing or running start.

■ Enslaved African gold miners were forbidden from speaking, so they communicated using percussive taps and stomps. This has evolved into a unique form of gumboot dance.

■ Wellington boots are also called gumboots because in New Zealand they were made from gum rubber.

■ In 1972, Paddington Bear started to wear wellington boots.

■ The largest wellington boot race involved 3,194 people in Ireland in 2014.

■ In 2017, Damian Thacker completed a marathon wearing wellington boots in 3 hours, 21 minutes and 27 seconds. This is the fastest on record in wellington boots.

Ready

■ **Key resources**: *Where My Wellies Take Me* by Michael and Clare Morpugo (2012) (Activity 1); wellies, bricks or wooden/polystyrene blocks, buckets of mud, trowels (Activity 2); wellies, shoe boxes, stands, cards numbered 1–10 (Activity 3).

■ **Health and safety**: ensure that children stand at a safe distance if arranging a welly wanging competition. Provide reminders of classroom rules during visits.

■ **Key vocabulary**: walk, jump, hop, run, throw, splash, rubber.

Steady

Before teaching, reflect on the following goals/learning intentions:

■ To read and understand simple sentences.

■ To listen attentively to stories.

■ To count numbers in order to 10.

Go

Activity 1: Where will your wellies take you?

Read *Where My Wellies Take Me* by Michael and Clare Morpugo (2012), which tells the story of Pippa who stays with her aunt in the countryside and loves going for walks in her wellies. Discuss the different wildlife and people that Pippa encounters. Where might the children's wellies take them? Read some of the poems aloud together, and create your own class versions based on your local area.

Activity 2: Builders

Wellies are, of course, great for playing in the mud. For this activity, the children can build their own brick and mud walls, wearing wellies to keep their toes safe and hard hats and visibility vests to complete the part. Look closely at a wall in the local environment and get the children to talk about the shapes they can see. Set out a number of small bricks (these can be real bricks, wooden blocks or polystyrene ones), and give the children a bucket of mud and some trowels. They can stack the bricks, slathering a layer of mud onto each one, and then use their trowels to scrape off the excess.

Activity 3: Shoe shop

Arrange the role play area of the classroom into a shoe shop using shoe boxes, stands and cards numbered 1–10 next to the relevant size of boot. Model serving customers and meeting their different needs – for example, what size boots will a baby need? How many boots will be needed if two children come into the shop needing new boots? What questions do the shopkeeper assistants need to ask their customers?

Other ideas

■ **Take the children on a visit to a local shoe shop wearing their wellies**: record interesting things on the journey by taking digital photographs and add these to a class map. Explore using a digital camera zoom feature to take close-up shots of wellies and display these on the map too. Write a sentence underneath: 'My wellies took me to …' Do the children recognise the owners from the boots?

■ **On a rainy day, take the children into the playground and ask them to move through puddles in different ways wearing their wellies**: for example, walking slowly, running, hopping, walking backwards, on one leg, walking in small steps, stretching.

■ **Arrange for the children to take part in their own welly wanging competition**: how far can they throw a welly? How can they measure the distance? How can they make sure it is a fair competition?

Find out more

■ Read the story of *The Girl Who Loved Wellies* by Zehra Hicks (2012) about a little girl, Molly, who loves her wellies so much that she never takes them off. Use the story to stimulate discussion about what the children love to wear and why.

X is for X-rays

In a nutshell

In 1895, Wilhelm Röntgen, a German professor of physics, invented the X-ray by accident. He was experimenting with how to conduct electricity when he discovered a mysterious ray capable of lighting up a fluorescent screen a few metres away. When he waved his hand between the ray and the screen, he saw a shadow of his own bones. Röntgen was then able to replace the screen with a photographic plate – and for the first time it was possible to peer inside the human body.

Within weeks, European doctors were using the technology to look for bullets and other foreign objects in the human body. X-rays were also used to diagnose fractures and gunshot wounds. Röntgen was understandably awarded the Nobel Prize in physics for his contribution to science.

However, it was not until the 1900s that the health risks associated with X-rays became known. Thomas Edison's assistant, Clarence Dally, who had worked extensively with X-rays, died of skin cancer in 1904.

Despite this, X-rays have been a huge advance. They have enabled scientists to treat cancer, look into space and understand the structure of DNA – what makes us unique as humans. Art historians use X-rays to find 'underpaintings' – rough sketches painters once drew to guide their work.

Did you know?

■ The X in X-ray is the mathematical symbol for unknown.

■ The first X-ray featured a woman's hand (Anna Bertha was the wife of Wilhelm Röntgen). When she saw the image showing her skeletal fingers, she exclaimed: 'I have seen my death!'

■ US shoe shops had X-ray machines fitted in the 1940s and 1950s to ensure a better fit.

■ The smallest possible point that an X-ray beam can focus on is between 20 and 30 nanometres (in comparison, a full stop is 1 million nanometres in diameter).

■ In 2009, the X-ray was named the most important modern scientific discovery by nearly 50,000 people in a Science Museum of London poll.

■ Among the items that have showed up on X-rays of people have been: a SpongeBob Squarepants pendant, a live grenade, an engagement ring and a candy cane.

Ready

■ **Key resources**: X-rays or images of X-rays of a variety of body parts (Activity 1); X-rays, black paper, craft materials (Activity 2); modelling clay, plaster of Paris (Activity 3).

■ **Health and safety**: plaster of Paris can be a very useful resource, but care must be taken in its use – avoid contact with the eyes and skin. Adults should be the ones to pour, etc.

■ **Key vocabulary**: X-ray, doctor, hospital, bones, joints, body parts.

Steady

Before teaching, reflect on the following goals/learning intentions:

■ To develop narratives and explanations by connecting ideas and events.

■ To make observations of living things.

■ To safely use and explore a variety of materials, tools and techniques.

Go

Activity 1: X-ray examination

Talk with the children about whether they have ever had an X-ray, or if they have ever been to an airport and seen the X-ray scanners. Source X-rays or print images of X-rays from online sites. Discuss what X-rays show and look closely at the bones. Which part of the body do they think they can see? What are the names of the bones? Are they surprised what some bones look like? Can they sort and match the X-rays with pictures of body parts? Can they arrange them into a body shape and name the parts? Include some X-rays of animals to extend the discussion.

Activity 2: 3D X-rays

Encourage the children to look closely at an X-ray of a hand and discuss what they can see. How many bones are there in a thumb? What shapes are the different bones? Get the children to draw around each other's hands onto black paper and help them to cut out the hands. Use a range of materials such as cotton buds, straws, modelling clay and paper to recreate the bones on paper and display these in the class 'X-ray department'.

Use modelling clay to make impressions of hands, feet, elbows and so on. Look closely at the impressions before filling them with plaster of Paris. After this has dried and set, remove the modelling clay and look at the moulds. Can they identify the body parts? Can they compare them with their friends' bodies? Decorate the models.

Other ideas

- **Parts of the body bingo**: create a series of bingo cards with parts of the body on them (e.g. head, fingers, foot, mouth). Depending on the children these may be words, pictures or a combination of the two. Create matching sets of cards and play the bingo game. Adapt to have a game of body part snap.

- **Labelling the body parts**: Crickweb (http://www.crickweb.co.uk/ ks1science.html) has a drag-and-drop activity for young children where body parts can be dragged onto the correct part of a photograph. This activity gives feedback as to whether the child has put the labels in the right places and is free to download.

Find out more

- Books such as *Jessica's X-Ray* by Pat Zonta (2002) or *Charlie is Broken!* by Lauren Child (2009) can be useful starting points for a discussion about broken bones. There are also many non-fiction books about doctors, such as *Doctor* (People Who Help Us) by Amanda Askew (2009).

- The BBC's Schools website includes activities for young children about 'Ourselves': http://www.bbc.co.uk/schools/scienceclips/ages/5_6/ ourselves.shtml.

Y is for Yoghurt Pots

In a nutshell

Yoghurt is at least 5,000 years old. It was first made by goatherds, in what is now Turkey, who fermented milk in sheep skin bags to conserve it. The first yoghurt 'pots' were made of animal stomachs. The natural enzymes curdled the milk, producing what we now call yoghurt.

In the 1970s, frozen yoghurt was first introduced in New England. In 2017, Onken launched for a limited time the first ever personalised yoghurts which allowed consumers to choose three of their favourite combinations out of a choice of twelve, including pumpkin, mint, mango, carrot and rhubarb.

Yoghurt is not only a food. For centuries, it has been used as a natural moisturiser to revitalise dull, dry skin. Yoghurt also contains 'good' bacteria which help to regulate food digestion and prevent problems such as gas and bloating.

Yoghurt pots are made from polystyrene. Although it is costly to recycle them into other products via mixed plastic recycling facilities, they can be used around the house and garden – for example, as plant pots and paint/glue pots.

Did you know?

- The Turkish word *yoghurt* means 'to condense or thicken'.

- According to the journal *Prevention*, Greek yoghurt has two times as much protein as regular yoghurt.

- In ancient Greek myths, ambrosia was the food of the Gods and yoghurt was one of the ingredients which symbolised strength and immortality.

- In 2009, a row broke out when Marks and Spencer used the US spelling 'yogurt' (without the 'h') on its pots.

- In 2014, the MP Brandon Lewis was corrected by his wife when he said that you could recycle yoghurt pots. (It is possible but very expensive.)

- Strawberry is the most popular yoghurt flavour according to a recent Yoplait survey.

Ready

- **Key resources**: yoghurt, soft fruit, vanilla essence, honey, bowl, mixing spoon, freezer (Activity 1); yoghurt, shallow bowls, icing pens, decorations (e.g. berries, chocolate buttons) (Activity 2); images of breakfasts from around the world, a range of breakfast foods (Activity 3); large slices of fruit (e.g. watermelon, apple, pear), berries, yoghurt, plates, small cookie cutters, artwork involving food (Activity 4).

- **Health and safety**: ensure good hygiene when preparing and eating food. Remain sensitive to individual circumstances when talking about food eaten at home (reports suggest that many children may not have eaten breakfast[1]). Check for allergies before preparing food.

---

1 Four in five teachers report children coming to school without having had breakfast: see Coughlan (2012).

■ **Key vocabulary**: mix, stir, add, ingredients, healthy, enjoy, like/don't like.

Steady

Before teaching, reflect on the following goals/learning intentions:

■ To name a range of different foods, and talk about whether they are healthy or not.

■ To use 'I like …' and 'I don't like …' to express preferences.

■ To recognise, create and describe patterns.

■ To know about similarities and differences between themselves and others, and among families, communities and traditions.

■ To represent their own ideas through art, exploring a variety of materials.

Go

Activity 1: Strawberry yoghurt ice cream

This is a very simple recipe, suitable for young children to make, which will help them to learn about measuring, mixing and freezing. You will need 3 cups of Greek yoghurt, 1 teaspoon of vanilla essence, a squeeze of lemon juice, ¼ cup of honey, 1 cup of diced strawberries (or other soft fruit). Stir all the ingredients (except the strawberries) together in a bowl, then add the diced strawberries. Let the mixture freeze for two to four hours. For children with specific dietary requirements other yoghurts can be used (e.g. coconut yoghurt).

Activity 2: Yoghurt designs

In Japan, yoghurt is used (in very shallow bowls) as the canvas for creative artwork. Encourage the children to practise mark making by allowing them to use icing pens to write on their yoghurt or to explore pattern by adding fruit shapes to the yoghurt bowl.

Can they copy a pattern that you give them? Can they create their own? Can they use increasingly controlled fine motor skills to decorate their yoghurt? Machiko Tateno, a cooking expert who teaches yoghurt art, suggests that as well as promoting healthy eating, it is also very relaxing.

Activity 3: Best breakfasts

Talk to the children about what they enjoy eating for breakfast. How many of them eat yoghurt? Cereal? Fruit? Provide them with paper plates and ask them to draw or find pictures of their favourite foods to put on the plates. Discuss whether their best breakfast is the same as their friend's. Talk about how in different countries people enjoy many different foods. Look at images available online about breakfast around the world (e.g. http://www. neatorama.com/neatolicious/2014/03/13/What-Do-People-around-the-World-Eat-for-Breakfast or http://cookingtheglobe.com), but remain aware that these may contain generalisations and stereotypes. Ask the children to look for similarities and differences between their breakfast and other breakfasts. They could interview parents and friends about their favourite breakfast foods. Plan different tasting sessions so the children can try various foods, such as different types of bread. This may provide a good opportunity to develop some home–school links, and parents/carers may be willing to come in and talk about their traditional breakfast foods.

Activity 4: Fruity artwork

Take large slices of fruit such as watermelon, apple or pear, and ask the children to arrange them on a plate. Talk about shape, texture, smell and colour. Encourage the children to use small cookie cutters to remove shapes from the slices – such as hearts, stars or circles – and then fill in the gaps using yoghurt, berries, etc. to create beautiful pieces of fruit art. Extend to look at the work of artists such as Giuseppe Arcimboldo (1526–1593), who painted images of fruit and vegetables to create unusual portrait paintings. Or look at the work of more contemporary artists such as Carl Warner and create pictures inspired by his food art.

Other ideas

■ **Favourite yoghurt flavours**: carry out some taste tests of a range of different yoghurts and then conduct a survey of the children's favourite flavours. Use pictures of the yoghurt pots to display the results in a visual graph. Talk about how they know which flavour was most popular.

■ **Invent a new yoghurt**: use a simple yoghurt flavour as a base, such as vanilla or strawberry. Design and create a new flavour, and use exciting vocabulary to describe it, such as 'Berrylicious Blueberry Burst'. Look at the packaging of yoghurts and design a suitable pot for the new flavour. For the more adventurous, design something for a favourite book character, such as 'Honey Syrup Porridge' flavour yoghurt for Goldilocks. *Roald Dahl's Revolting Recipes* (1997) can provide some more disgusting inspiration!

Find out more

■ Yoghurt pots have all kinds of uses around the house. Repurpose them into resealable containers for buttons and other craft materials, blocks, small world people or Scrabble letters. You can use an old yoghurt container as a mould for lollies. The website This Old House has ideas for reusing old yoghurt cups: https://www.thisoldhouse.com/ideas/10-uses-yogurt-cups. These include cutting a small hole in the bottom of a cup, slipping a paintbrush through it and using the cup to catch drips as you are painting. They can also be used to sow seeds (just make sure you drill some holes in the bottom first), or use them as sand toys or shovels/containers in the water play area. Lots of crafting ideas using pots can be found on sites such as Pinterest.

■ The British Council has a set of resources about food around the world: https://esol.britishcouncil.org/sites/default/files/attachments/informational-page/Unit%203_Food%20around%20the%20world.pdf.

■ Find more recipes using yoghurt at: https://www.foodnetwork.com/recipes/articles/50-things-to-make-with-yogurt.

Z is for Zebra-Patterned Fabric

In a nutshell

Animal-inspired fabric prints have been popular for more than 200 years. Across Europe, the houses of the gentry were stocked with rugs, curtains and wall hangings featuring animal designs. They were liked because animals projected power, authority and exotic qualities.

Films have done much to popularise the use of animal fabrics in the home. In 1932, *Tarzan the Ape Man* featured animal print costume designs. As a result, leopard and cheetah print fabrics became popular among film stars. Films such as *Mrs Robinson* (1968) also brought animal prints to the attention of millions.

Lots of fabrics are produced from animals, and this offers opportunity for some moral debate. These include cashmere which comes from the

Himalayan goat, felt from rabbits' fur and mohair from the angora goat. However, the most widely used are woollen carpets, feather pillows and leather suites. Alternative and more ethical plant-based fibres include cotton, linen, denim and rayon. Polyester fleece is a popular alternative to wool.

Medieval people did not like looking at stripes because they found that they disturbed their view of background and foreground colours. Stripes were once associated with evil and seen as the cloth of the devil. Slaves, servants and convicts were all dressed in striped clothes. By Victorian times, striped fabrics had become more fashionable. Queen Victoria dressed her son in a sailor suit, and swimming costumes were made of navy blue and white stripes. The striped flags of France and the United States were also popular.

Did you know?

- The word zebra is believed to come from the Latin *equiferus*, which means 'wild horse'.

- It was once believed that zebras were white animals with black stripes, whereas they are in fact black animals with white stripes!

- The stripes on every zebra are unique.

- There are a number of different zebra species and subspecies. The plains zebra is the most common and the Grévy's zebra, of Kenya and Ethiopia, is the rarest. It is officially classified as endangered.

- The zebra's stripes are an example of camouflage, making it difficult to focus on when moving and thus making it harder to catch.

- The zebra has inspired lots of different fabric designs, such as pink zebra, snow zebra, bright rainbow watercolour zebra, zebra gathering and running purple zebras. See: https://www.spoonflower.com/tags/zebra.

■ There are many famous zebras, such as Marty the zebra in the *Madagascar* films. However, many would say that the most famous zebra of all is to be found in Abbey Road, London. This is not an equine, but a zebra crossing, immortalised by the Beatles.

Ready

■ **Key resources**: *We're Going on a Lion Hunt* by David Axtell (1999), resources such as buckets of water, swampy trays, etc., images/videos of African landscapes and animals, lion footprints, African animal puppets (Activity 1); plastic animals, number cards, toy animals (Activity 2); holiday brochures, video clips of African animals in the wild, photos of African peoples and hot air balloons, large cardboard box, role play props such as binoculars, cameras and telescopes (Activity 3); Julia Ocker's short film *Zebra* (available online), zebra prints, black and white paint, zebra-shaped paper templates (Activity 4).

■ **Health and safety**: take appropriate care when re-enacting the story in Activity 1 or moving independently around the provision.

■ **Key vocabulary**: stripes, patterns, animal names (e.g. zebra, lion, rhinoceros, elephant, hippopotamus, cheetah), Africa, safari, watch, long, sticky, fierce, teeth, roar, float, watch, tiptoe.

Steady

Before teaching, reflect on the following goals/learning intentions:

■ To follow instructions involving several ideas or actions.

■ To answer 'how' and 'why' questions in response to stories or events.

■ To show good control and coordination in large and small movements.

■ To count reliably from 1 to 20.

■ To know about similarities and differences between themselves and others and among communities and traditions.

Go

Activity 1: *We're Going on a Lion Hunt*

Talk about the animals that live in Africa and look at photographs and videos. David Axtell's *We're Going on a Lion Hunt* (1999) is an adaptation of the famous *We're Going on a Bear Hunt* book by Michael Rosen (1989). Talk about the front cover. What might this book be about? What animals might they find in this story? Read the story to the children. What do they like about the story? Which is their favourite bit? Discuss the events that occur. Can the children recall any parts of the story in their own words? Set up your provision to allow re-enactment of the story. Use imagination and clever resources, such as those used in the live action stage performance of *We're Going on a Bear Hunt* (https://www.youtube.com/watch?v=3kw4j8noltU), to represent the swamp, lake and grass. Or create a puppet theatre retelling of the story. Or use musical instruments to add a soundtrack to the story. Place lion foot-prints in the provision and allow the children to dress up as explorers and follow these, tiptoeing, running and crawling from place to place.

Activity 2: Number safari

Place a large collection of plastic African safari animals in a box, and tell the children that there are some mystery creatures inside. Invite them to explore the animals, using touch first and guessing what they might be, then looking closely at them and naming them. Ask each child in turn to make a set of two or three animals that are the same in some way. Ask them to explain the connections (perhaps they all eat meat or they all have spots). Repeat this several times, and encourage other children to guess and predict the con-nections. Next, hide other toy animals throughout the provision, such as three lions or five giraffes – the children are going on a number safari. Give them a numeral card and an animal card. Ask them to find that number of hidden animals. Extend by providing written clues for some or simple oral instructions for others. The children could take photos of the animals when they have been found and use these to make a safari number line.

Activity 3: African safari

Bring a range of holiday brochures for safaris into the class. Show the children pictures of people on safari. Talk about their clothes and the types of vehicles in which they travel. Explain that a safari is a journey to spot and photograph wild animals, such as lions and elephants. Show videos of African animals in the wild and describe how safaris offer a chance to watch the animals in their natural homes rather than in a cage at a zoo. Explain how important it is to watch the animals quietly and not to disturb them. How could they do this? Talk about hot air balloons and show photographs of these, and discuss what the occupants might see from the basket if they were on safari in Africa. Create a role play balloon basket from a large cut-down cardboard box and provide binoculars, cameras and telescopes for an imaginary safari journey. Provide objects for the children to select to take on a safari to pack in their safari rucksack. What might they need? Consider building a safari campfire in the outdoor provision, adding hammocks and tents if there is space to do so. Predict some of the people they might see – such as the Maasai. Talk about skin and hair colour, hairstyles and jewellery (e.g. hair ornaments, necklaces, earrings) and discuss similarities and differences sensitively.

Activity 4: Zebra patterns

Julia Ocker's short film about a zebra whose pattern keeps changing is a good starting point for exploration of pattern: https://www.youtube.com/watch?time_continue=104&v=n5yn7V5QOAE. Watch the film and talk about whether they recognise some of the patterns they have seen. Provide the children with templates of zebras and black and white paints. What sort of patterns can they produce? Can they describe their patterns? Can they repeat and extend the pattern across the whole zebra?

Other ideas

■ **Zebra, zebra, lion**: change the wording of the familiar 'duck, duck, goose' game to fit a zebra theme. Sit the children in a circle. One child walks around and gently pats other children on the head saying 'zebra' or 'lion'. If they say 'lion', that child has to get up and race the picker around the circle. The first one back sits down and play continues with the child still standing becoming the picker.

■ **Houses and homes**: source a range of pictures of different homes from around the world (e.g. flats, houses, caravans, castles, tents, huts, shacks, boats, igloos), focusing particularly on the different countries in Africa. Look closely at these pictures of homes. What can the children see? What do they think the houses have been made from? Can they compare their own bedrooms and those of children in other countries, noting any similarities or differences? Encourage the children to describe their own homes and to say why they like to live in them. This could be extended to look at animal homes.

Find out more

■ Many charities have educational resources available – for example, Send a Cow has 'Lessons from Africa' with many classroom resources such as African recipes and games: http://www.sendacow.org.uk/lessonsfromafrica.

■ Contact local zoos to see if visits are possible. Zoos are not without controversy, so ensure that any visits are to those recognised for high quality animal care and conservation. The British and Irish Association of Zoos and Aquariums has a website: http://www.biaza.org.uk/education/schools-downloads. If this is not possible, use images and videos from animals in the wild, such as those produced by the BBC Natural History Unit.

Conclusion

Throughout this book, we have adopted a view that values young children as capable, sociable and curious learners. It is very much in keeping with the Reggio Emilia approach to educating young children, where teachers use a stimulus known as a 'provocation' (Thornton, 2014). These provocations can take different forms, such as questions, events (e.g. a holiday) and objects. They are designed as open-ended activities without prescribed outcomes. The intention is to stimulate children's thinking, discussion, questions, ideas and interests. Both teacher and child play an active role in the learning process. The teacher takes a deliberate and thoughtful decision regarding the materials, media and general direction of the learning, and the child is allowed the time and space to take the ideas where they want. Through the use of different sources of provocation, the child can develop creativity, inventiveness, flexible thinking and reflection (Honegger, 2018). Provocations can be as simple as a photograph of a rock sculpture next to some pebbles, or as elaborate as a table with an assortment of recycled materials next to a book on robots and resources to make upcycled robots. Often, though, provocations are simple and displayed beautifully to provoke interest.

Objects are valuable teaching resources because they are not age specific and neither do they demand a certain level of literacy or numeracy skills for children to be able to contribute to lessons. In Part 2, we have suggested around 200 activities to stimulate young children's thinking around everyday objects. These can be adapted to suit the different needs of your children and are not meant to be taken as a unit of work. Although the focus for this book has been on the under-sevens, the principle of providing first-hand learning experiences and opportunities to explore and question apply to older children too.

Our focus has been on the four C's of communication, collaboration, critical thinking and creativity (see Appendix). Many of the activities involve opportunities for children to develop their communication skills in authentic contexts. For example, children can respond to stories related to objects, listen to the views of others and carry out simple research to find out more information. We have also highlighted the importance of providing children with a range of materials, tools and scenarios to stimulate their creativity, which, of course, goes beyond the traditional arts. Most of the suggested activities can be undertaken in small groups which enables children to gain experience and confidence in talking to others, taking turns and negotiating understanding. Finally, we have stressed the importance of not underestimating the potential for critical thinking among young children. Many of the activities allow teachers the opportunity to extend thinking skills, such as reasoning, problem solving and evaluating.

In our experience of working with practitioners in many different early years settings, it is possible to enthuse, engage and challenge young children's thinking by using familiar objects as starting points, without buying expensive resources. Teaching effectively on a shoestring is aided by the rise of discount shops where teachers can source many of the resources featured in this book cheaply. We have also drawn attention to natural resources and experiences that generations of young children have enjoyed, irrespective of age, school location, prior experience or stage of development.

While we have highlighted the use of everyday objects, one of the goals of education is to extend children's horizons beyond the familiar so they are introduced to new experiences. This means equipping children with the knowledge, skills and dispositions so they are able to look at things afresh. Everyday objects are a means to this end. They are starting points for children to think about the value of objects, past and present, their cultural significance in different societies and the environmental implications of the stuff that surrounds us. Above all, objects should be viewed as a bridge to other people, places and times.

Appendix: Mapping activities against the 4 C's

The focus of this book has been on how the use of everyday objects can support the development of the 4 C's (communication, collaboration, critical thinking and creativity). As a quick guide, the following table maps each activity against the four C's in terms of the main focus of the task.

Of course, the activities we suggest are just starting points, so depending on how they are adapted in individual contexts the focus can change. The age and developmental level of the children will impact on the nature of the task and the focus. All activities will have an element of communication associated with them. Many also contribute to other curriculum areas, such as mathematical development and knowledge and understanding of the world.

Letter	Activity	Page number	Main focus			
			Communication	Collaboration	Critical thinking	Creativity
A	1. Apple tasting	52	X		X	
	2. Make apple art	53				X
	3. Cook with apples	53	X	X	X	
	4. Visit an allotment, orchard or garden	53	X		X	
B	1. Don't pop me!	58	X		X	
	2. Try to make me a square	58	X		X	
	3. A bubble in a bubble in a bubble	58			X	
	4. Bubble caterpillars	59		X		X
C	1. Which box next?	63			X	
	2. Packing parcels	64				X

Letter	Activity	Page number	Main focus			
			Communication	Collaboration	Critical thinking	Creativity
	3. Deconstruction engineer	64	X	X		
	4: Drive-in movie	64		X		X
D	1. Personalised books	70	X			
	2. Signs and symbols	70	X		X	
	3. That's me in the picture	70	X			X
	4. Mix and match	71		X		X
E	1. Egg decorator	76				X
	2. Word family fun	76	X			X
	3. Egg box number recognition	76	X		X	
	4. Eggsellent recipes	77	X	X		
	5. How long is a minute?	77		X	X	
F	1. Peacock sculptures	81				X
	2. Feather mosaic	82	X			X
	3. Banquets for birds	82		X	X	X
	4. Talking pieces	82	X			X
G	1. Fizzy fun	87	X		X	
	2. Smoothie superstore	88	X	X	X	X
	3. Races in a glass	88	X		X	
	4. Clay sculpture	89				X
H	1. Hula hoop circus	92		X		X
	2. Hoopla	93			X	
	3. Number wheels	93	X	X		

Letter	Activity	Page number	Main focus			
			Communication	Collaboration	Critical thinking	Creativity
	4. Hoop weaving	93				X
I	1. Flower, leaf and berry building blocks	97	X		X	X
	2. Melting is messy	98	X		X	
	3. Ice pictures	98			X	X
	4. Set me free	98	X		X	
J	1. Jam jar cookery	102	X	X		X
	2. Honey bee dance	103	X	X		X
	3. Flight of the Bumblebee	103	X		X	X
	4. Programming a Bee-Bot	104	X	X	X	
K	1. Zoom in on *The Kite*	108	X		X	
	2. Chinese kites	109			X	X
	3. Windsock	109				X
	4. Wind chimes	109			X	X
L	1. Journey sticks	113	X		X	X
	2. Leaf plates and bowls	114			X	X
	3. Natural art gallery	114	X			X
	4. Giant nest	115	X	X		X
M	1. Map of the classroom	119	X			X
	2. High above	119	X		X	
	3. Maps, maps, maps	120	X		X	
N	1. Never-ending notebook	124	X	X		X
	2. Nature's notebook	124	X		X	X

Letter	Activity	Page number	Main focus			
			Communication	Collaboration	Critical thinking	Creativity
	3. Mix 'n' match notebook	125	X		X	X
	4. Go anywhere notebook (and writing belt)	125	X			X
O	1. Whose porridge is this?	129			X	
	2. Give Goldilocks some advice	130	X		X	
	3. Where are the bears?	130	X	X		
	4. Order the bears	130			X	X
P	1. *The Toymaker*	134	X			
	2. Making peg dolls	134				X
	3. Washing lines	135	X		X	
Q	1. Money, money, money	138			X	
	2. Mini enterprisers	138	X	X	X	X
	3. Designing coins and stamps	139				X
	4. *The Jolly Postman*	139	X			X
R	1. Rock and fossil museum	143	X			X
	2. Make your own fossils	143				X
	3. Dinosaur egg hunt	144	X	X	X	X
S	1. Exploring old shoes	148	X		X	
	2. Hang out the washing	149			X	
	3. Comparing feet	149	X			
	4. Footprints	149	X		X	X
T	1. Exploring old phones	154	X		X	
	2. Help!	154	X			

Letter	Activity	Page number	Main focus			
			Communication	Collaboration	Critical thinking	Creativity
	3. Talk, talk, talk	154	X			X
U	1. Whose umbrella?	158		X	X	
	2. Making your own umbrella	158			X	X
	3. Rainy day songs	158	X			
V	1. Windy washing lines	162	X			
	2. Wash basket	162	X		X	
	3. How strong is Velcro?	163			X	
W	1. Where will your wellies take you?	166	X			X
	2. Builders	166	X			X
	3. Shoe shop	167		X	X	
X	1. X-ray examination	170	X		X	
	2. 3D X-rays	170				X
	3. Moulding body parts	171				X
Y	1. Strawberry yoghurt ice cream	174	X			
	2. Yoghurt designs	174			X	X
	3. Best breakfasts	175	X		X	
	4. Fruity artwork	175				X
Z	1. We're Going on a Lion Hunt	180	X		X	X
	2. Number safari	180	X		X	X
	3. African safari	181	X	X	X	X
	4. Zebra patterns	181	X		X	X

Endnotes

The facts and figures mentioned in the 'In a nutshell' and 'Did you know?' sections are drawn largely from the Guinness World Records (www.guinnessworldrecords. com) and established media sources such as the BBC, along with museums and the respective websites listed for each entry.

A is for Apples

https://www.telegraph.co.uk/news/uknews/8446634/Britains-favourite-apples.html

https://www.telegraph.co.uk/foodanddrink/healthyeating/11171530/Why-we-are-eating-the-
    wrong-kind-of-apples.html

https://www.ncbi.nlm.nih.gov/pmc/articles/PMC2664987

http://www.agribenchmark.org/agri-benchmark/did-you-know/einzelansicht/artikel//
    a-quarter-of.html

https://www.foodforlife.org.uk

http://www.childrensfoodtrust.org.uk

https://www.foodinschools.org

B is for Bubbles

https://pubs.acs.org/cen/whatstuff/stuff/8117sci3.html

https://recordsetter.com/world-record/people-pop-bubblewrap-once/3677

https://recordsetter.com/world-record/hand-bubbles-blown-minute/46296?autoplay=false

http://www.guinnessworldrecords.com/world-records/largest-free-floating-soap-bubble

http://www.recordholders.org/en/list/soapbubbles.html

C is for Cardboard Boxes

https://www.campaignlive.co.uk/article/kellogg-odds-sainsburys-cereal-packaging/1029124

http://www.diamondpak.co.uk/corrugated-packaging-facts

https://www.theage.com.au/news/News/Out-of-the-box/2005/06/07/1118123836379.html

http://www.toyhalloffame.org/toys/cardboard-box

https://www.valreas.net/musee.html

https://www.linkedin.com/pulse/
    how-many-cardboard-boxes-does-amazon-ship-each-day-david-perlman

http://www.guinnessworldrecords.com/world-records/largest-cardboard-box

D is for Digital Cameras and Digital Photographs

http://www.bbc.co.uk/news/magazine-16483509

http://uk.businessinsider.com/12-trillion-photos-to-be-taken-in-2017-thanks-to-smartphones-
    chart-2017-8

http://www.guinnessworldrecords.com/world-records/
    most-self-portrait-photographs-(selfies)-taken-simultaneously

https://recordsetter.com/world-record/
    photographs-ones-self-taken-from-birth-sixteen-years-age/36260?autoplay=false

http://www.dailymail.co.uk/sciencetech/article-3619679/What-vain-bunch-really-24-billion-selfies-
    uploaded-Google-year.html

https://www.telegraph.co.uk/technology/11881900/More-people-have-died-by-taking-selfies-this-
    year-than-by-shark-attacks.html

E is for Eggs, Egg Timers and Egg Boxes

https://eggbox.com/history-egg-packaging/

https://www.standard.co.uk/news/uk/national-trust-makes-uturn-on-banning-easter-from-cadbury-
    egg-hunt-after-previous-years-scandal-a3777806.html

https://www.telegraph.co.uk/news/newstopics/howaboutthat/7309852/Hen-lays-giant-egg.html

http://www.guinnessworldrecords.com/world-records/largest-egg-and-spoon-race

http://www.guinnessworldrecords.com/world-records/smallest-bird-egg

http://www.guinnessworldrecords.com/world-records/largest-chocolate-easter-egg

http://www.guinnessworldrecords.com/
    world-records/96971-most-creme-eggs-eaten-in-one-minute

https://www.winstonswish.org/
    winstons-wish-and-hundreds-of-soldiers-celebrate-after-becoming-world-record-breakers

http://www.arlingtoncemetery.net/charles-bendire.htm

F is for Feathers

http://www.guinnessworldrecords.com/world-records/first-feathered-animal

http://www.guinnessworldrecords.com/world-records/largest-vocabulary-for-a-bird-living

http://www.guinnessworldrecords.com/world-records/oldest-duck

http://www.guinnessworldrecords.com/
    world-records/106300-most-canned-drinks-opened-by-a-parrot-in-one-minute

http://www.guinnessworldrecords.com/world-records/largest-dreamcatcher

G is for Glasses (and Goblets)

https://www.britannica.com/biography/George-Ravenscroft

http://www.vam.ac.uk/content/articles/t/the-crystal-palace

https://www.telegraph.co.uk/news/earth/3313930/Is-it-worth-it-Recycling-glass.html

http://www.guinnessworldrecords.com/world-records/387255-largest-plastic-cup-pyramid

H is for Hoops

http://www.hulahooping.com/history.html

http://www.guinnessworldrecords.com/world-records/longest-time-to-hula-hoop-underwater

http://www.guinnessworldrecords.com/world-records/longest-marathon-hula-hooping

http://www.recordholders.org/en/list/hulahoop.html

http://www.guinnessworldrecords.com/
world-records/23744-most-hula-hoops-spun-simultaneously

I is for Ice Cubes

https://nsidc.org/cryosphere/glaciers/quickfacts.html

http://www.icecreamhistory.net/frozen-dessert-history/ice-cream-timeline

https://www.icehotel.com/about-icehotel

https://www.livescience.com/32641-whats-the-worlds-biggest-glacier.html

https://www.nbcnews.com/science/
scientists-say-otzi-iceman-has-living-relatives-5-300-years-8C11392771

http://ocean.si.edu/ocean-photos/one-hundred-names-sea-ice

J is for Jam Jars

https://www.telegraph.co.uk/news/9558240/Not-so-much-jam-tomorrow-as-spread-falls-out-of-fashion.html

https://www.nesta.org.uk/news/guide-historical-challenge-prizes/french-food-preservation-prize

https://www.dalemain.com/winners-2018-marmalade-awards-announced

https://duerrs.co.uk/5k-jar-of-marmalade

http://www.athens-times.com/greece/
the-most-expensive-honey-in-the-world-costs-as-much-as-a-small-car/

K is for Kites

https://kites.com/history-of-kites

https://www.fi.edu/benjamin-franklin/kite-key-experiment

http://www.dailymail.co.uk/news/article-2718877/Biggest-kite-world-wows-crowds-China.html

http://www.kiteman.co.uk/DidYouKnow.html

L is for Logs (and Leaves)

https://www.nature.com/articles/nature14967

http://www.go-nagano.net/shisetsu-detail?shisetsuid=6022004

https://earthobservatory.nasa.gov/Features/ForestCarbon

https://earthobservatory.nasa.gov/Features/Deforestation/tropical_deforestation_2001.pdf

http://science.sciencemag.org/content/342/6160/850

https://www.ppec-paper.com/thousand-new-tree-seedlings-planted-every-minute-canada

http://cfs.nrcan.gc.ca/pubwarehouse/pdfs/35191.pdf

http://wwf.panda.org/wwf_news/?uNewsID=207367

M is for Maps

https://www.ancient.eu/image/526

https://www.bl.uk/collection-items/britannia

https://www.telegraph.co.uk/news/6415598/Englands-oldest-map-goes-on-sale.html

https://www.ordnancesurvey.co.uk/about/overview/history.html

https://www.geolounge.com/map-orientation

https://www.loc.gov/item/prn-03-110/
    library-completes-purchase-of-waldseemuller-map/2003-06-18

N is for Notebooks

https://www.artofmanliness.com/2010/09/13/the-pocket-notebooks-of-20-famous-men

https://www.theguardian.com/artanddesign/jonathanjonesblog/2013/feb/12/
    leonardo-da-vinci-notebooks-art

https://www.nytimes.com/1989/04/23/business/the-executive-computer-a-sprightly-porta-
    ble-but-flawed.html

http://www.simonandschuster.com/books/The-Perfection-of-the-Paper-Clip/
    James-Ward/9781476799865

https://www.independent.co.uk/arts-entertainment/books/features/moleskine-a-page-out-of-al-
    tered-history-7870099.html?origin=internalSearch

http://www.guinnessworldrecords.com/news/commercial/2016/5/
    nuco-international-unveils-largest-notebook-ever-at-london-stationary-show-427489

O is for Oatmeal

https://www.jordanscereals.co.uk/news/a-short-history-of-porridge

http://www.quakeroats.com/about-quaker-oats/content/quaker-history.aspx

https://www.ncbi.nlm.nih.gov/pubmed/21631511

https://www.independent.co.uk/life-style/food-and-drink/instant-porridge-sachets-pots-not-
    healthy-breakfast-sugar-quantities-diet-quaker-oats-nairns-rude-a7566981.html

https://www.marysmeals.org.uk

https://www.telegraph.co.uk/news/uknews/1447181/Footman-exposes-Tupperware-secret-of-the-
    Queens-table.html

P is for Pegs

https://medium.economist.com/the-curious-history-of-the-clothespeg-3f8615519c61

http://www.guinnessworldrecords.com/world-records/most-clothes-pegs-held-in-the-hand

https://www.phrases.org.uk/meanings/342950.html

http://www.guinnessworldrecords.com/world-records/largest-clothes-peg

Q is for Queen's Head

http://www.nationalarchives.gov.uk/education/resources/the-royal-seal

https://www.postalmuseum.org/discover/explore-online/postal-history/penny-black

http://www.bbc.co.uk/news/uk-12144444

https://www.royalmint.com/discover/sovereigns/the-1953-sovereign

https://www.royalmint.com/discover/royalty/the-royal-portraits

https://www.morningadvertiser.co.uk/Article/2017/10/23/Most-popular-pub-names-in-the-UK-2017

https://www.telegraph.co.uk/news/2017/03/28/
     revealed-new-1-coins-hidden-security-feature-works

http://www.bbc.co.uk/newsround/39816967

http://www.wired.co.uk/article/new-one-pound-coin-uk-release-details-security

R is for Rocks (and Pebbles)

https://www.nps.gov/moru/index.htm

S is for Shoes (and Socks)

https://www.vam.ac.uk/shoestimeline

https://www.pepysdiary.com/diary/1660/01/22/

http://www.northamptonshirebootandshoe.org.uk/content/category/
     story-of-an-industry/a-proud-heritage

https://www.northampton.gov.uk/homepage/273/the_history_of_shoes

T is for Telephones

http://www.bbc.co.uk/timelines/zfyfy4j

https://www.btplc.com/Thegroup/BTsHistory/index.htm

https://www.smithsonianmag.com/smart-news/
     first-telephone-book-had-fifty-listings-and-no-numbers-180962173

http://www.businessinsider.com/the-evolution-of-the-cell-phone-2013-1?IR=T

http://www.dailymail.co.uk/wires/pa/article-5420089/Britons-receive-33-800-mobile-phone-
     messages-year.html

https://www.theguardian.com/theguardian/from-the-archive-blog/2012/jun/29/
     archive-1937-first-999-call

https://www.ofcom.org.uk/about-ofcom/latest/media/media-releases/2012/
     uk-is-now-texting-more-than-talking

https://www.independent.co.uk/news/uk/home-news/mobile-phones-drivers-guilty-convicted-
     wheel-plummets-decline-rac-traffic-officers-a8204726.html

http://home.bt.com/tech-gadgets/
     mr-watson-come-here-i-want-to-see-you-from-patent-disputes-to-queen-victoria-the-amazing-
     history-of-the-telephone-11364044754021

https://www.telegraph.co.uk/news/uknews/2117112/Telephone-manners-die-out-as-children-
     abandon-hello-greeting.html

https://www.bbc.co.uk/bbcthree/article/d1c23412-3043-429e-a00b-5d997a2f6f83

http://latvia.eu/news/new-guinness-world-record-latvia-longest-telephone-conversation

https://www.independent.co.uk/life-style/gadgets-and-tech/news/there-are-officially-more-mobile-
     devices-than-people-in-the-world-9780518.html

https://www.archives.gov/presidential-libraries/events/centennials/nixon/exhibit/nixon-online-exhibit-calls.html

https://www.huffingtonpost.co.uk/entry/kids-mobile-phones-activities_uk_5a708015e4b05836a2569da0

U is for Umbrellas

http://www.umbrellahistory.net

http://www.bbc.co.uk/news/av/magazine-37376130/the-bbc-journalist-assassinated-with-a-poison-tipped-umbrella

https://www.newyorker.com/magazine/2008/02/11/thinking-in-the-rain

http://www.guinnessworldrecords.com/news/commercial/2015/7/nfb-members-refuse-to-let-blindness-define-them-by-seizing-their-umbrellas-and-a-387529

http://www.guinnessworldrecords.com/world-records/largest-umbrella-parasol

https://www.mirror.co.uk/news/world-news/worlds-biggest-umbrella-dance-10000-3424170

V is for Velcro (and Buttons and Zips)

https://www.velcro.co.uk/about-us/history

https://www.livescience.com/34572-velcro.html

http://journals.plos.org/plosone/article?id=10.1371/journal.pone.0011331

W is for Wellington Boots

http://www.english-heritage.org.uk/learn/story-of-england/georgians/invention-wellington-boot

https://www.telegraph.co.uk/culture/11465309/Best-Duke-of-Wellington-facts.html

https://dancehistorygumbootdancing.weebly.com/narrative.html

https://www.paddington.com/us/infos/faqs

http://www.guinnessworldrecords.com/world-records/largest-wellington-boot-race

http://www.guinnessworldrecords.com/world-records/112581-fastest-marathon-wearing-wellington-boots

X is for X-rays

http://mentalfloss.com/article/70900/9-transparently-amazing-facts-about-x-rays

http://iopscience.iop.org/article/10.1088/1742-6596/808/1/012010/meta

https://www.telegraph.co.uk/news/science/science-news/6498941/X-ray-voted-most-important-modern-discovery.html

Y is for Yoghurt Pots

http://blogs.discovermagazine.com/scienceandfood/2017/07/04/the-science-of-yogurt/#.Wt8AHJch2Uk

https://www.thegrocer.co.uk/buying-and-supplying/new-product-development/onken-teams-up-with-food-designers-for-personalised-yougurts/557178.article

https://www.prevention.com/food/healthy-eating-tips/what-greek-yogurt

http://mentalfloss.com/article/63073/12-tangy-facts-about-yogurt

https://www.telegraph.co.uk/news/newstopics/howaboutthat/5388116/Row-erupts-over-yoghurt-producers-using-American-spelling.html

http://www.bbc.co.uk/news/uk-politics-27680027

https://www.ranker.com/list/best-yoplait-flavors-v1/ranker-food

Z is for Zebra-Patterned Fabric

https://www.greenhousefabrics.com/blog/history-animal-print-exotic-past-revealed

https://valentinagurarie.wordpress.com/tag/the-devils-cloth-a-history-of-stripes-and-striped-fabric

https://www.aol.com/article/news/2016/03/28/the-truth-behind-whether-zebras-are-black-or-white/21334610

http://www.discoverwildlife.com/animals/mammals/10-amazing-zebra-facts

References

Ahlberg, J. and Ahlberg, A. (1986) *The Jolly Postman, or Other People's Letters*. London: William Heinemann.

Alexander, R. (2005) *Towards Dialogic Teaching: Rethinking Classroom Talk*. York: Dialogos.

Alvarado, A. E. and Herr, P. R. (2003) *Inquiry-Based Learning Using Everyday Objects*. Thousand Oaks, CA: Corwin Press.

Anderson, L. W. and Krathwohl, D. R. (eds) (2001) *A Taxonomy for Learning, Teaching, and Assessing: A Revision of Bloom's Taxonomy of Educational Objectives*. New York: Longman.

Anning, A. and Edwards, A. (eds) (2006) *Promoting Children's Learning from Birth to Five*. Maidenhead: Open University Press.

Askew, A. (2009) *Doctor* (People Who Help Us). London: QED Publishing.

Aston, D. H. (2012) *A Rock Is Lively*. San Francisco, CA: Chronicle Books.

Axtell, D. (1999) *We're Going on a Lion Hunt*. London: Macmillan Children's Books.

Baker, S. M. and Gentry, J. W. (1996) 'Kids As Collectors: A Phenomenological Study of First and Fifth Graders', in K. P. Corfman and J. G. Lynch Jr (eds), *NA – Advances in Consumer Research, Volume 23*. Provo, UT: Association for Consumer Research, pp. 132–137.

Bandura, A. (1976) *Social Learning Theory*. Harlow: Pearson.

Beloglovsky, M., Daly, L. and Gonzalez-Mena, J. (2016) *Loose Parts 2: Inspiring Play with Infants and Toddlers*. St Paul, MN: Redleaf Press.

Birkby, Robert and Boy Scouts of America (1990) *The Boy Scout Handbook: The Trail to Eagle*, 10th edn. Irving, TX: Boy Scouts of America.

Bloom, B. S., Engelhart, M. D., Furst, E. J., Hill, W. H. and Krathwohl, D. R. (1956) *Taxonomy of Educational Aims: Classification of Educational Objectives. Handbook I: Cognitive Domain*. New York: David McKay.

Blott, U. (2016) 'Incredible 4D Ultrasound Scans Show What Foetuses REALLY Get up to in the Womb', *Daily Mail* (17 February). Available at: http://www.dailymail.co.uk/femail/article-3449559/Detailed-4D-ultrasound-scans-babies-really-womb.html.

Bond, M. (1958) *A Bear Called Paddington*. London: Collins.

Bourn, D., Hunt, F., Blum, F. and Lawson, H. (2016) *Primary Education for Global Learning and Sustainability*. York: Cambridge Primary Review Trust.

Bradman, T. (1989) *The Sandal*. London: Andersen Press.

Brewster, C. and Fager, J. (2000) *Increasing Student Engagement and Motivation: From Time on Task to Homework*. Portland, OR: Northwest Regional Educational Laboratory.

Brown, B. (2001) 'Thing Theory', *Critical Inquiry*, 28(1) (autumn), 1–22.

Bruner, J. S. (1960) *The Process of Education*. Cambridge, MA: Harvard University Press.

Bryant-Mole, K. (1998) *Where is Marmaduke?* London: Evans Brothers.

Cabrera, J. (2017) *There Was an Old Woman Who Lived in a Shoe*. New York: Holiday House.

Carle, E. (2015) *Brown Bear Treasury*. London: Puffin.

Carlton, M. P. and Winsler, A. (1998) 'Fostering Intrinsic Motivation in Early Childhood Classrooms', *Early Childhood Education Journal*, 25(3), 159–166.

Cassidy, S. (2017) 'School Leavers Lack Basic Work Skills, CBI Warns', *The Independent* (3 July). Available at: https://www.independent.co.uk/news/education/education-news/school-leavers-lack-basic-work-skills-cbi-warns-9582458.html.

Council for the Curriculum, Examinations and Assessment (CCEA) (2006) *Understanding the Foundation Stage.* Belfast: CCEA.

Council for the Curriculum, Examinations and Assessment (CCEA) (2007) *The Northern Ireland Curriculum: Primary.* Belfast: CCEA.

Chatterjee, H. J. and Hannan, L. (2016) *Object-Based Learning in Higher Education.* London: Ashgate.

Chiarotto, L. (2011) *Natural Curiosity: A Resource for Teachers.* Ontario: Ontario Institute for Studies in Education, University of Toronto.

Child, L. (2009) *Charlie is Broken!* St Louis, MO: Turtleback Books.

Clearabee (2015) 'UK Homes Hoard £259 Billion Junk Mountain' (21 May). Available at: https://www.clearabee.co.uk/news/uk-homes-hoard-259-billion-junk-mountain/.

Coe, R., Aloisi, C., Higgins, S. and Major, L. E. (2014) *What Makes Great Teaching? Review of the Underpinning Research.* London: Sutton Trust.

Conley, D. T. (2007) *Toward a More Comprehensive Conception of College Readiness.* Eugene, OR: Educational Policy Improvement Center. Available at: https://docs.gatesfoundation.org/documents/collegereadinesspaper.pdf.

Cooper, T. (ed.) (2010) *Longer Lasting Products: Alternatives to the Throwaway Society.* Abingdon: Routledge.

Coughlan, S. (2012) 'Parents "failing to give children breakfast" ', *BBC News* (16 October). Available at: http://www.bbc.co.uk/news/education-19951590.

Craft, A. (2000) *Creativity Across the Primary Curriculum: Framing and Developing Practice.* London: Routledge.

Dahl, R. (1997) *Roald Dahl's Revolting Recipes.* Harmondsworth: Puffin.

Daily Mail (2013a) 'Do You Have £1,000 of Clutter in Your Home? Study Finds Average Household is Sitting on Unused Items Worth a Small Fortune' (19 March). Available at: http://www.dailymail.co.uk/news/article-2295537/Do-1-000-clutter-home-Study-finds-average-household-sitting-unused-items-worth-small-fortune.html.

Daily Mail (2013b) 'Hello Baby! Incredible 3D Scans Allow Parents to See Foetus SMILING and MOVING in Stunning Detail' (29 March). Available at: http://www.dailymail.co.uk/sciencetech/article-2300983/Incredible-3D-scans-allow-parents-foetus-SMILING-MOVING-stunning-detail.html.

Davies, J. A. and Pestell, T. (2015) *A History of Norfolk in 100 Objects.* Stroud: History Press.

Davis, A. (2012) 'Forget Buying Must-Have Toys, Give the Kids a Box for Christmas', *Evening Standard* (30 October). Available at: https://www.standard.co.uk/news/health/forget-buying-must-have-toys-give-the-kids-a-box-for-christmas-8252929.html.

Department for Children, Schools and Families (DCSF) (2009) *Learning, Playing and Interacting – Good Practice in the Early Years Foundation Stage.* London: DCSF.

Department of Education for Northern Ireland (DENI) (2013) *Learning to Learn: A Framework for Early Years Education and Learning.* Bangor: DENI. Available at: https://www.education-ni.gov.uk/sites/default/files/publications/de/a-framework-for-ey-education-and-learning-2013.pdf.

References

Diamandis, P. H. and Kotler, S. (2012) *Abundance: The Future Is Better Than You Think*. New York: Free Press.

Eaude, T. (2012) *How Do Expert Primary Classteachers Really Work?* Plymouth: Critical Publishing.

Early Education (2012) *Development Matters in the Early Years Foundation Stage (EYFS)*, London: Early Education.

Education Scotland (2016) *A Statement for Practitioners from HM Chief Inspector of Education*. Livingston: Education Scotland. Available at: https://www.eis.org.uk/Content/images/education/Curricular%20Guidance/cfestatement.pdf.

Ellacott, S. E. (1968) *A History of Everyday Things in England*. Vol. V: *1914–1968*. London: Batsford.

Flanders, J. (2014) *The Making of Home: The 500-Year Story of How Our Houses Became Our Homes*. London: Atlantis Books.

Flood, A. (2013) 'Are Children's Books Reinforcing Materialism?', *The Guardian* (22 April). Available at: https://www.theguardian.com/books/2013/apr/22/children-books-reinforce-materialism-claims-research.

Flournoy, V. (1985) *The Patchwork Quilt*. New York: Penguin.

Gabot, M. and Fair, L. (2012) *Emily and the Rainbow Umbrella*. N.p.: Brainy Connections.

Gervais, R. (2004) *Flanimals*. London: Faber & Faber.

Goodman, A., Joshi, H., Nasim, B. and Tyler, C. (2015) *Social and Emotional Skills in Childhood and Their Long-Term Effects on Adult Life*. London: Institute of Education.

Gosling, S. (2009) *Snoop: What Your Stuff Says About You*. London: Profile Books.

Goss, J. and Tribe, S. (2016) *Doctor Who: A History of the Universe in 100 Objects*. London: Random House.

Gravett, E. (2011) *Orange, Pear, Apple, Bear*. London: Macmillan Children's Books.

Griffiths, N. (2008) *Walter's Windy Washing Line*. Swindon: Red Robin Books.

Grigg, R. (2015) *Becoming an Outstanding Primary Teacher*. Abingdon: Routledge.

Grigg, R. (2016) *Big Ideas in Education: What Every Teacher Should Know*. Carmarthen: Crown House Publishing.

Grigg, R. and Hughes, S. V. (2013) *Teaching Primary Humanities*. Harlow: Pearson.

Grigg, R. and Lewis, H. (2016) *An A–Z of Outdoor Learning*. London: Bloomsbury.

Hanson, W. (2015) 'How Posh Are YOU? The 15 Household Items Only the Upper Middle Classes Own Revealed in Our Quiz (and the 10 Things You Should Never Buy)', *Daily Mail* (8 April). Available at: http://www.dailymail.co.uk/femail/article-3030119/How-posh-15-household-items-upper-middle-classes-revealed-quiz-10-things-never-buy.html.

Harford, T. (2007) *The Undercover Economist*. London: Abacus Books.

Harrod, H. (2014) 'Are These the Most Important Objects of Our Time?', *The Telegraph* (21 June). Available at: https://www.telegraph.co.uk/culture/art/art-features/10892924/Are-these-the-most-important-objects-of-our-time.html.

Hegley, J. (2011) *Stanley's Stick*. London: Hodder Children's Books.

Hicks, Z. (2012) *The Girl Who Loved Wellies*. London: Two Hoots.

Hissey, J. (1986) *Old Bear*. London: Penguin.

Hogben, M. (2007) *101 Antiques of the Future*. London: New Holland.

Hohmann, M. and Weikart, D. P. (1995) *Educating Young Children*. Ypsilanti, MI: HighScope Educational Research Foundation.

Honegger, D. S. (2018) 'Designing Free Choice Play Centers with Provocations', *Journey Into Early Childhood* [blog] (31 January). Available at: http://www.journeyintoearlychildhood.com/journey-into-pre-k-and-k-blog/designing-free-choice-play-centers-with-provocations.

Inkpen, M. (1987) *One Bear at Bedtime*. London: Hodder Children's Books.

Jenkins, M. (1999) *The Emperor's Egg* (Read and Wonder). London: Walker Books.

Jones, G. V. I. and Martin, M. (2006) 'Primacy of Memory Linkage in Choice Among Valued Objects', *Memory and Cognition*, 34(8), 1587–1597.

Jopson, M. (2015) *The Science of Everyday Life: Why Teapots Dribble, Toast Burns and Light Bulbs Shine*. London: Michael O'Mara.

Kavanagh, G. (2000) *Dream Spaces: Memory and the Museum*. Leicester: Leicester University Press.

Kerr, J. (1972) *Mog the Forgetful Cat*. London: HarperCollins Children's Books.

Kim, K. H. (2011) 'The Creativity Crisis: The Decrease in Creative Thinking Scores on the Torrance Tests of Creative Thinking', *Creativity Research Journal*, 23(4), 285–295. Available at: http://www.nesacenter.org/uploaded/conferences/SEC/2013/handouts/Kim_Creativity-Crisis_CRJ2011.pdf.

Kolirin, L. (2014) 'Britain's Secret Hoarding Habit Revealed', *Daily Express* (6 March). Available at: https://www.express.co.uk/news/weird/463357/Britain-s-clutter-is-worth-32-7-billion-according-to-the-British-Heart-Foundation.

Lewis, H. (2013) 'Developing a Shared Culture of Thinking in the Early Years', *Wales Journal of Education*, 16, 37–53.

Lindsey, B. (2008) *The Age of Abundance: How Prosperity Transformed America's Politics and Culture*. New York: HarperCollins.

MacVean, M. (2014) 'For Many People, Gathering Possessions Is Just the Stuff of Life', *Los Angeles Times* (21 March). Available at: http://articles.latimes.com/2014/mar/21/health/la-he-keeping-stuff-20140322.

Mansour, D. (2005) *From Abba to Zoom: A Pop Culture Encyclopedia of the Late 20th Century*. Kansas City, MO: Andrews McMeel Publishing.

Marks, H. M. (2000) 'Student Engagement in Instructional Activity: Patterns in the Elementary, Middle and High School Years', *American Educational Research Journal*, 37(1), 153–184.

Mason, T. (2017) *Bears!* N.p.: CreateSpace.

Matusiak, J. (2016) *The Tudors in 100 Objects*. Stroud: History Press.

McCartney, J. (2013) 'Make Do and Mend? Nothing Is Built to Last Any More', *The Telegraph* (10 August). Available at: https://www.telegraph.co.uk/finance/property/green/4304957/Make-do-and-Mend-Restoring-the-good-things-in-life.html.

Mercer, N. (2000) *Words and Minds. How We Use Language to Think Together*. Abingdon: Routledge.

Morpurgo, M. and Morpurgo, C. (2012) *Where My Wellies Take Me*. Dorking: Templar Publishing.

Mortimer, G. (2012) *A History of Cricket in 100 Objects*. London: Profile Books.

Moss, A. and Skinner, K. (2015) *Scotland Yard's History of Crime in 100 Objects*. London: History Press.

National Literacy Trust (2005) *Why Do so Many Children Lack Basic Language Skills? A Discussion Paper Prepared by the Talk to Your Baby Campaign*. London: National Literacy Trust.

Nicholson, S. (1971) 'How Not to Cheat Children – The Theory of Loose Parts', *Landscape Architecture*, 62, 30–35.

O'Toole, F. (2013) *A History of Ireland in 100 Objects*. Royal Irish Academy.

Ockleford, A. (2002) *Objects of Reference*. London: RNIB.

Ormerod, P. (2016) 'Believe It or Not, Brits Are Becoming Less Materialistic', *The Guardian* (26 December). Available at: https://www.theguardian.com/commentisfree/2016/dec/26/britain-less-materialistic-consuming-less-sharing-more.

Paris, S. G. (2002) *Perspectives on Object-Centred Learning in Museums*. Mahwah, NJ: Taylor & Francis.

Partnership for 21st Century Learning (P21) (2016) *Framework for 21st Century Learning*. Washington, DC: P21. Available at: http://www.p21.org/storage/documents/docs/P21_framework_0816.pdf.

Pickthall, B. (2012) *A History of Sailing in 100 Objects*. London: Bloomsbury.

Plate, B. (2015) *A History of Religion in 5½ Objects: Bringing the Spiritual to Its Senses*. Boston, MA: Beacon Press.

Quennell, C. and Quennell, M. (1918) *A History of Everyday Things in England*. Vol. 1: *1066–1499*. London: Batsford.

Raschka, C. (2015) *A Ball for Daisy*. New York: Schwartz & Wade.

Retail Gazette (2013) 'Number of UK Consumers Willing to Pay More for Eco-Friendly Products Triples in 17 Months' (22 August). Available at: https://www.retailgazette.co.uk/blog/2013/08/14142-number-of-uk-consumers-willing-to-pay-more-for-ecofriendly-products-triples-in-17-months.

Rickinson, M., Dillon, J., Teamey, K., Morris, M., Choi, M. Y., Sanders, D. and Benefield, P. (2004) *A Review of Research on Outdoor Learning*. London: NFER/Kings College London.

Ritchhart, R. (2002) *Intellectual Character: What It Is, Why It Matters, and How to Get It*. San Francisco, CA: Jossey-Bass.

Robinson, K. (2009) *The Element: How Finding Your Passion Changes Everything*. London: Allen Lane.

Robinson, H. and Sharatt, N. (2005) *Mixed Up Fairy Tales*. London: Hodder Children's Books.

Robson, R. (2012) *Usborne Doodle Pad for Boys*. Oxford: Usborne Publishing.

Robson, R. (2012) *Usborne Doodle Pad for Girls*. Oxford: Usborne Publishing.

Rogers, P. and Rogers, E. (1992) *Our House*. London: Walker Books.

Rogoff, B. (1991) *Apprenticeship in Thinking: Cognitive Development in Social Context*. Oxford: Oxford University Press.

Rosen, M. (1989) *We're Going on a Bear Hunt*. London: Walker Books.

Rowlands, M. (2008) 'The Elderly as "Curators" in North London', in E. Pye (ed.), *The Power of Touch: Handling Objects in Museum and Heritage Context*. Abingdon: Routledge, pp. 139–152.

Royal National Institute of Blind People (RNIB) (2014) *Communication: Complex Needs*. London: RNIB.

Royal Society for the Protection of Birds (RSPB) (2006) *Out-of-Classroom Learning: Practical Information and Guidance for Schools and Teachers*. London: RSPB.

Royte, E. (2008) *Bottlemania: How Water Went on Sale and Why We Bought It*. London: Bloomsbury.

Sanders, P. (1985) 'Enthusiasm Awareness in the Experiential Classroom', *Developments in Business Simulation & Experiential Exercises: Proceedings of the Annual ABSEL Conference,*

Volume 12. Available at: https://absel-ojs-ttu.tdl.org/absel/index.php/absel/article/viewFile/2163/2132.

Save the Children (2015) *Ready to Read.* London: Save the Children. Available at: https://www.savethechildren.org.uk/content/dam/global/reports/education-and-child-protection/ready-to-read-wales.pdf.

Scardamalia, M. (2002) 'Collective Cognitive Responsibility for the Advancement of Knowledge', in B. Smith (ed.), *Liberal Education in a Knowledge Society.* Chicago, IL: Open Court, pp. 67–98.

Schlechty, P. C. (2011) *Engaging Students: The Next Level of Working on the Work.* San Francisco, CA: Jossey-Bass.

Schwartz, B. (2005) *The Paradox of Choice: Why More Is Less.* New York: Harper Perennial.

Schweinhart, L. J., Montie, J., Xiang, Z., Barnett, W. S., Belfield, C. R. and Nores, M. (2005) *Lifetime Effects: The HighScope Perry Preschool Study Through Age 40.* Ypsilanti, MI: HighScope Press.

Scottish Government (2008) *Curriculum for Excellence. Building the Curriculum 3.* Edinburgh: Scottish Government.

Seefeldt, C. (2004) 'Helping Children Communicate', *Early Childhood Today,* 19(1), 36–42.

Sherman, J. (2004) *Shapes in the Sky: A Book About Clouds.* Mankato, MN: Picture Window Books.

Shulman, L. S. (1987) 'Knowledge and Teaching: Foundations of the New Reform', *Harvard Educational Review,* 57(1), 1–22.

Siraj-Blatchford, I., Sylva, K., Muttock, S., Gilden, R. and Bell, D. (2002) *Researching Effective Pedagogy in the Early Years.* London: Department for Education and Skills.

Smithers, R. (2016) 'British Households Fail to Recycle a "Staggering" 16m Plastic Bottles a Day', *The Guardian* (15 October). Available at: https://www.theguardian.com/environment/2016/oct/15/british-households-fail-to-recycle-a-staggering-16m-plastic-bottles-a-day.

Standards & Testing Agency (2018) *Early Years Foundation Stage Profile: 2018 Handbook.* London: Standards & Testing Agency.

Strasser, S. (2000) *Waste and Want: A Social History of Trash.* New York: Owl Books.

Stronge, J. H., Tucker, P. D. and Hindman, J. L. (2004) *Handbook for Qualities of Effective Teachers.* Alexandria, VA: Association for Supervision and Curriculum Development.

Surowiecki, J. (2005) *The Wisdom of Crowds: Why the Many Are Smarter Than the Few.* London: Abacus.

Taylor, B. and Tilford, D. (2000) 'Why Consumption Matters', in J. B. Schor and D. Holt (eds), *The Consumer Society Reader.* New York: New Press, pp. 463–487.

Telegraph, The (2010) 'Ten-Year-Olds Have £7,000 Worth of Toys but Play with Just £330' (20 October). Available at: https://www.telegraph.co.uk/finance/newsbysector/retailandconsumer/8074156/Ten-year-olds-have-7000-worth-of-toys-but-play-with-just-330.html.

Thomas, M. (2009) *Think Community: An Exploration of the Links between Intergenerational Practice and Informal Adult Learning.* London: National Institute of Adult Continuing Education.

Thornton, L. (2014) *Bringing the Reggio Approach to Your Early Years Practice.* Abingdon: Routledge.

References

Trajectory (2012) *The Ribena Plus Play Report*. Available at: https://trajectorypartnership.com/reports-and-presentations/report-1/.

Trentmann, F. (2016) *The Empire of Things: How We Became a World of Consumers, from the Fifteenth Century to the Twenty-First*. New York: HarperCollins.

Trilling, B. and Fadel, C. (2009) *21st Century Skills: Learning for Life in Our Times*. San Francisco, CA: Jossey-Bass.

Vecchi, V. (2010) *Art and Creativity in Reggio Emilia: Exploring the Role and Potential of Ateliers in Early Childhood Education*. Abingdon: Routledge.

Vygotsky, L. (1962) *Thought and Language*. Cambridge, MA: MIT Press.

Vygotsky, L. (1978) *Mind in Society: The Development of Higher Psychological Processes*. Cambridge, MA: MIT Press.

Waddell, M. (1993) *The Toymaker: A Story in Two Parts*. London: Walker Books.

Wainwright, O. (2014) 'The V&A Looks Outwards: Its Rapid Response Collecting Gallery Is Unveiled', *The Guardian* (2 July). Available at: https://www.theguardian.com/artanddesign/2014/jul/02/victoria-and-albert-rapid-response-gallery-unveiled.

Walker, R. and Glenn, J. (eds) (2012) *Significant Objects*. Seattle, WA: Fantagraphics.

Walsh, G., Murphy, P. and Dunbar, C. (2010) *Thinking Skills in the Early Years: A Guide for Practitioners*. Belfast: Stranmillis University College.

Ward, J. (2014) *The Perfection of the Paper Clip: Curious Tales of Invention, Accidental Genius, and Stationery Obsession*. New York: Simon & Schuster.

Watkins, L., Aitken, R., Robertson, K. and Williams, J. R. (2016) 'Advertising's Impact on Pre-Schoolers' Brand Knowledge and Materialism', *International Journal of Consumer Studies*, 40(5), 583–591.

Watt, F. (2010) *Animal Doodles* (Usborne Activity Cards). Oxford: Usborne Publishing.

Weidman, A. C. and Dunn, E. W. (2016) 'The Unsung Benefits of Material Things: Material Purchases Provide More Frequent Momentary Happiness Than Experiential Purchases', *Social Psychological and Personality Science*, 7(4), 390–399.

Welsh Government (2015) *Foundation Phase Framework*. Cardiff: Welsh Government. Available at: http://learning.gov.wales/docs/learningwales/publications/150803-fp-framework-en.pdf.

Willingham, W. W., Pollack, J. M. and Lewis, C. (2002) 'Grades and Test Scores: Accounting for Observed Differences', *Journal of Educational Measurement*, 39(1), 1–37.

Womack, S. and Petre, J. (2008) 'Rowan Williams: Children Are "Too Materialistic"', *The Telegraph* (26 February). Available at: https://www.telegraph.co.uk/news/uknews/1579887/Rowan-Williams-Children-are-too-materialistic.html.

World Economic Forum (2016) *New Vision for Education: Fostering Social and Emotional Learning through Technology*. Geneva: World Economic Forum. Available at: http://www3.weforum.org/docs/WEF_New_Vision_for_Education.pdf.

Wright, S. (2010) *Understanding Creativity in Early Childhood: Meaning-Making and Children's Drawings*. London: Sage.

Zonta, P. (2002) *Jessica's X-Ray*. Toronto: Firefly Books.

Acknowledgements

We would like to thank all the students and teachers who have so willingly tried out our suggestions and shared their own ideas. We are particularly grateful to Emma Tuck, Rosalie Williams, Tabitha Palmer and Tom Fitton at Crown House Publishing for their excellent guidance through the publication journey. Any errors remain our own.

Finally, our thanks go to our respective parents (Jack, Mildred and Dilys) and our children (Grace, Sofie, Tom and Mia). They have all made us think about the importance of early childhood and the values that really matter.